How to Order Chinese During a Hostage Crisis

Dialects, Existential Essays, A Play, and Other Poems

Hog Press

Joseph D. Reich

Hog Press
922 5th Street
Ames, IA 50010
USA
www.hogpress.com

editor@hogpress.com

Hog Press

How To Order Chinese During A Hostage Crisis: Dialects, Existential Essays, A Play, And Other Poems. Copyright © 2017 by Joseph D. Reich. All rights reserved.

No part of this book may be reproduced in any form by any electronic or mechanized means (including photocopying, recording, or information storage and retrieval) without written permission, except in the case of brief quotations embodied in critical articles and reviews.

For more information, please visit www.hogpress.com

ISBN-10:   0-9848942-9-2
ISBN-13:   978-0-9848942-9-1

Cover design by polytekton.com
Drawing courtesy of Dylan Reich ©2017

Contents

Dialects…	8
The Land Of Beaurocrats (and how to sell mouthwash)…	10
One Of Those Affairs…	12
Breaking Down The Principle Of 'Free Will And Volition' From An Existential, Empirical, And Psychological Model…	13
On The Concept Of Damage –for Charles Bukowski…	16
On The Subject Of Surrealism…	17
A Didactic List Of Ghosts…	20
The Natural Instincts, Configurations, Choreography And Choruses Of Evolution…	22
Cops & Robbers (and the healing power of snow)…	24
Right Around That Nightclub Adam's Apple…	25
One Of Those Moods…	26
Somewhere Right Around Then…	33
Time Warped…	34
Psych!...	36
Rolling Dice In The Bones Of Paradise…	37
1969, Los Angeles…	39
Phoenix…	40
For Gregory Corso & Holden Caufield…	41
A Strange Way Of Looking At Things…	42
Price Chopper…	43
On The Nature Of Weather (sci-fi vs. suicide)…	44
4 Reasons To Become An Expatriate…	45
A Brunch For Strangers…	46
Making A Self For Your Name…	47
For William Carlos Williams Physician From Patterson…	48
Just Like Chuck Norris & Christey Brinkley…	49
The Loneliest Man In The World…	51
Yeshiva…	52
No Translation…	53
That Song "Landslide"…	55
Bittersweet Aphorisms Of The Seasons: With Your Own Free Additional Guide For Survival…	57
That Leftover Gold Dust In The Parking Lot Of Early Dusk…	104
The Hx Of Mankind & Civilization…	105
Working Methadone…	106
A Different Sorr Of Autobiography…	107
Swallowing Your Pride Chasing It With Something Even More Depressing…	109
Bewitching Hour Or Time Of Prayer…	111
Fish & Wildlife…	112
Myths: 101 Easy Installments Of Pomp & Circumstance…	113
Eulogy In Ebonics…	163

Something Like Chocolate Milk & Grilled Cheese…	165
A Declarative Question…	166
Fast Food…	167
A Bio Of Gertrude Stein & Alice B. Toklas…	168
Scenic Route…	169
Pain Scale…	170
Configurations…	171
The Symbolism Of Nightmares…	172
True (or false positive)…	173
Please Follow Directions…	174
Life Sometimes Like Just Having Survived A Stoning…	175
Sanctuary: how all language turns to rhythm & cadences of the seasons…	176
The Tomboy Class…	177
Please Beware…	178
The Beginning And End Of That Film…	179
How To Celebrate Holidays Alone 3,500 Miles Away From Home…	181
Blues Or That Song By Billy Joel…	182
Paying Ransom With House Money: configurations, life-transitions & aphorisms…	183
The Criminal Life…	199
No Safe Place To Even Kill Yourself Anymore…	212
Pool Rules: The Life-Cycle (from a cognitive-behavioral perspective) Or A Darwinian Comparison Between The Animal Kingdom And Homo Sapien…	218
The Life & Times Of Bazooka Joe…	220
Something Like Radio Or The Hx Of The Black Dope Addict Floorwaxer Floating Around The Foyer…	223
Baileys Irish…	225
Parts Of Speech…	225
Vegas Way Before It Was Called Vegas…	230
Word Problems…	231
Zenith…	232
Silverware…	233
The Local Express…	235
The Old Country…	236
Blues Is Brooding 1:23 In The Afternoon Truly Having Nowhere To Go On 145th & Amsterdam In The Sweltering Summer…	237
Talk Therapy…	238
This Is A Wreck/ording…	239
A Different Sort Of Pillow Talk…	240
The Shape & Form Of Mist & Fog…	241
The Origins Of Billy The Kid…	242
A Portrait –for William Carlos Williams…	243
Bridesmaid (on suicide watch)…	244

Those Creaky Steps Of Growth & Development…	245
Social Work: don't be a stranger…	246
Progress Notes…	247
Axe Body Spray…	248
The Graveyard…	249
A Found Poem: America for $11.25 an hour…	250
Certain Such Elements…	253
Fall Foliage (or at the bottom of a box of crackerjacks)…	258
How To Survive & Cope The Overthrow Of A Government At One Of Those All-Inclusive Resorts…	259
Off Season…	260
A Life Lesson For One Of Those Life Lessons…	262
For Wittgenstein, H. Caufield, And Mark Twain…	263
For Louis-Ferdinand Celine…	265
The Difference Of Denouements…	266
Life On The Planet…	267
Earth: a short film or play in the vein of the theater of the absurd…	268
Numb: a short film called "human resources"…	269
A Sci-Fi Fable: somewhere between redtape blues & blackmail…	270
A Strange Sociological Axiom…	271
The True (falsehoods) Of Advertising…	272
Color Of Pool…	273
Triggers…	274
Saints And Other Odd Things…	275
Down & Out In The Montreal Mall…	276
Feeling Lost & Lonely In The Very Schmaltzy And Fancy-Schmantzy Tourist Streets Of Quebec City Turning To The Olympics On Your TV…	278
Crime & Punishment (American-Style)…	281
A Time Like That…	282
Amen:i:festo…	283
The Tourism Industry…	284
Ralph Lauren…	285
Art…	286
Missing Puzzle To The Peace…	287
Rush Hour (forecast)…	288
Domestic Violence Or Why White Trash Still Live With Their Mothers…	290
Not For Nothing…	293
Love, Exciting And New…	295
Sophistication…	296
American Existentialism…	297
The Holy Healing Scent Of Rain…	306
Scenes From The Sunshine State…	309
Scenes From Inside Plato's Cave…	310
Motels And Stars Some Where Behind The Smog…	312

Living Outside The Terrarium…	313
The Cognitive-Behavioral Makeup Of Ghosts…	315
Bells & Steeples & Graveyards…	320
Something Like Pillow Talk…	321
Okee-Dokey (Just Like Christ & Karaoke)…	323
Dreaming Of Splendor When You're Broke And Down On Your Luck…	324
Americana…	325

"I went to the place where every white face was an invitation to robbery"

-The Clash

Dialects

After a long train ride from Venice
I conclude splendor is deceiving

Or too much beauty has always left me
feeling lonely and empty and triggers
the nihilistic sensation of trepidation

Nodding-out on the veranda overlooking the decadent lake
in the very affluent mountains controlled by dictators
and old money and madmen and Mafioso

The wife gets into a stare down
with a dozen orthodox girls
on the funicular

She's so good looking and charming seduces
all the waiters on the lake and can get practically
anything she wants who return the favor by calling her
consistently, ridiculously, by the wrong formal last name
like Freudian slips of the tongue after his breakup with Jung

We get so bored out here and have some
money to spend take a ferry back and forth
which transports us from Italy to Switzerland
to pick up cheese and chocolate and brandy

I often have to save her terrycloth hat
which blows off her head in the breeze
and becomes something of a tradition
or a slapstick punchline without the riddle

We spend dusks wandering the cobblestone
for fresh Gelato with chunks of chocolate
mousse cake sticking out of them

Old men play chess with the gigantic figures
seeming temporarily contented with the misery
of what existence has brought them still fixated
by the will to win while ironically on the defensive

We get back just in time to the veranda
on the lake to take supper at sunset
and then sneak back just in time

before all the whining obnoxious
spoiled tourists come to spoil it

Sometimes I like to fantasize
about the innkeeper's wife who
presents as wise and insightful
and generous and kind while he's
never around and wonder why not
which subliminally touches on
the topic of virtue and vice

We make it back to our room
with those plumes of huge
white comforters and fall
back into them to catch
the international news

The ancient cathedral across the lake
which chimes on the hour like some
strangely familiar coo-coo is the only
thing which keeps us from feeling
lost and lonesome and abandoned

To know that marriage
is just a roll of the dice
somewhere between
the rituals of existence
and remains of advice
but better I guess than
going it alone in this life.

The Land Of Bureaucrats (or how to sell mouthwash)

I dreamt there was a ferry heading to America

and all there was was a drunk tug boat captain

with a lit skyline where I was denied entry...

There was a murder weapon and false witnesses

There were drag queens and flamboyant lounge singers in sequins

returning home exhausted after an evening on the beat

A thief carrying my set of *World Book Encyclopedias*

and little black book of women who refused to return my messages

An old dusty mannequin who plays piano in the window on Orchard

returning home down the cobblestone of palm readers

bailbondsmen and religious artifacts...

There was a hollering madwoman with a purse all full of stray cats

and her claim to fame that she used to once be Miss Coney Island

and if I asked her to marry her I'd be allowed to become a citizen

There was a glider circling overhead with a banner which read–

"Drink Schlitz Beer!"

Old solemn and sincere shirtless men with staticky transistors stuck to ears

and an endless boardwalk of gigolos, strumpets, blind men and stray dogs

An adorable little black boy eagerly probing and

asking inquisitive questions at the dynamite stand

Golden tenement prison castles silhouetted in shadows

and the closer you got to them the less familiar but more exotic

with stray scents of formaldehyde, orange rind, and pork fried rice

This is where the saints and organized crime come to die

A bike rack all filled with those old time Schwinn bicycles

with banana seats and gleaming Harley Davidson handlebars

and a young girl trying to seduce me with her skinned knees and

tomboy imagination which involved bullying and charming subjugation

A little further on I could see the customs agent

nodding out on heroin and felt like a new man...

One Of Those Affairs

At the out-of-town, out-of-town convention is where they meet

while their fellow cut-throat colleagues play business games

and exercises to test character, trust, integrity, and loyalty

blindly falling backwards into each others arms

standing face to face to see how comfortable

they feel with specific distance and space.

When they are telling their sadistic inside jokes

about having taken advantage of clients, quotas, and tax codes

two nondescript brokers deliberately not well-known manage to slip out into the hall.

Having secretly escaped it all, all you see in their very silent, plush hotel room

is makeup, medication, "Hello My Name Is..."

When they strip off their clothing they do so to rid themselves

of their identities, their realities, their suburbs, the states where they are from.

How they perform and get intimate is done through an opposite dynamic and function

as desperately, perversely, want to really get to know each other so go backwards

from pillow talk to climax to orgasm to build-up to arousal to seduction

to when their eyes originally met from across the ballroom.

Feelings cannot be hurt 'cause they stopped feeling ages ago.

Their room has a bird's-eye view of the beautiful desertion of days and seasons.

Of anonymity.

They check-out separately…

Breaking Down The Principle Of 'Free Will And Volition'
From An Existential, Empirical, And Psychological Model

    How strange and comforting to be dreaming of dreaming in my philosophy professor's bathroom with books piled high up to the ceiling, but unfortunately, due to the moirés and nature of the day, had to cope with the mundane games of a fellow colleague of mine, knocking vociferously, exclaiming the rules and regulations and that I was not allowed to, and brooded about rules and regulations but what for? For just taking advantage of a simple place to rest my bones? For the desire to experience the need and sensation to be left alone? For free thinking, as was finally at last having one of those good, self-soothing dreams where I was indeed happy and motivated, even aroused and turned on, consequently thus, started musing on the concept of what it meant to have free will and volition, and by this selfsame machination (or configuration and reasoning) posited, does one's own free will and volition really even exist at all?

    Or is not the essence of free will and volition the free will and volition to have free will and volition? To grasp at and get, or try to keep and maintain 'the spirit' (in feeling or emotion, or something collectively new, intuitive, and spontaneous) however specific, or simply its sensibility and aesthetic, whether just a part, or a whole collective variety of its elements which make up its existence? And in 'real life,' in fact, does it not often just result in its opposite(s)? Or is one's own free will and volition to no longer feel any sense of self-doubt, guilt, or conflict; no longer a victim to constant rhetoric and contradictions and others' quixotic defense-mechanisms (cognitive disconnects, 'convenient amnesia' or maddening configuration which often appears to separate people's language and semantics from their character and behavior, image and result from intentions, or morals and ethics from self-interest, manipulation and opportunism) and always leaves one 'confused and conflicted' (with inhibitions and resistance) consistently questioning one's place on earth and purpose in existence; to no longer strike out in bewilderment against their petty and pathetic semantics, impulsive and reactive? Or the abstract wish and dream and fantasy and seed of what we believe it is and means to be free? Is freedom maybe not just simply the dream and fantasy to finally somehow be 'left alone' without any boundaries, physically, emotionally, spiritually, or psychologically?

    I pictured all of my journeys in taking trains from place to place, town to town, city to city, region to region, country to country, dream to destiny, not knowing a living, breathing soul, even perhaps releasing my sudden sweet semen in the rattling bathroom with no forced expectations or pre-conceived notions (originally initiated by 'absurd' self-absorbed authority figures who could not possibly begin to know or never got to know a thing about my identity or personality) with a true sense of anonymity on my way to my unknown destiny, maybe high on some kind of hallucinogen or painkiller (lack of sleep and fatigue, providing a whole other type of instinct and adrenalin for the

senses) to 'naturally' liberate me from the absurd context and identity
and routine and ritual of my painful being; the crime of living…

    I reflected on spending blissful, adventurous days of wandering aimlessly through the streets of Monmartre, taking the TGV train from le Gare de Lyon, zooming through the opaque, industrial slums of Paris with the Mediterranean all of a sudden, miraculously showing up around the bend, and stepping in like some blissful madmen to the aromatic heat and humidity of the plane and palm trees of Nice (this sensation and phenomenon happening as well from Northern Spain to the fertile regions of Andalucia, and even The Deep South of The United States) my very first scene, experiencing and witnessing in my wrinkled linen suit, scooping succulent shrimp straight out the shell with a bottle of sparkling water on the beach, surrounded by reclining, topless ladies, gazing to the brilliant horizon where I would soon be crossing the border to Italy to take a ferry to the rugged beauty of Sicily;

    Getting released from Tombs in downtown Manhattan after being arrested, working the graveyard shift, hustling a yellow taxi in New York City, a literal 'mistaken identity' and being charged for 'resisting arrest' when simply asking (and not knowing) why he was stopping me, and that first feeling and sensation, like a revelation, of the fresh air and sun hitting me, ambling up the strange streets of beautiful, bleak Chinatown to make my way back to Brooklyn, having entered the spiritual realm of Kafka, Genet, and Dostoevsky, being inflicted with a sudden and unexplainable, quixotic subjugation and oppression, and then feeling and experiencing the cognitive and physiological phenomena of the elevated, fragile senses open (on the most surreal of levels) in what appeared like a new sight of beaming, bright, splashing light, and palpable forms and figures and scents and aromas (of what the scholar likes to so often refer to as a 'spiritual rebirth' after they unjustifiably take and violate and steal from you) then return your freedom (when their corrupt, systematic quota is through or have brutally 'paid your dues') also too, 'for no particular reason or explanation,' a literal 'slave to bureaucracy and the system' in a new and brilliant, keen and perceptive 'theater of the absurd.'

    I reminisced taking solitary, slow trains from Chicago through slums and smokestacks and silos to the lone figure of a beautiful, blushing, modest mother with her baby son at the crossroads, both enthusiastically waving with great pride and gusto (as if this was the only thing that mattered and in many ways was) at all the passing shadows which included myself, feeling my heart jump, while also being a part of, anonymous (autonomous…), yet perversely, some deep, keen feeling of belonging, and really didn't much matter where or which way we were going past the amorphous silhouettes of factories and industry, seeping together somewhere between the day and evening, off to Patterson, New Jersey, to that easy chair still sitting there, waiting there, broken and bare, exactly how I left it in the weeds of the Rastafarian courtyard of Avenue C in The Lower East Side beneath the stars, as I once more wondered if free will and volition really did exist at all, but not just more so a state of mind devoid of all those man-made, mandated, and manipulative things (smoke and mirrors) and stressors which make up time, relieved of those previous burdens which had at once

so brutishly 'kept me down,' keenly knowing and developing the wisdom and insight
of the fine line between that tangible state of flux and the 'ridiculous' obstacles and
'stuff' which separates the mundane routines and rituals of everyday existence with
those 'fleeting' moments which make up freedom when all that repeated suffering
(either empirical or existential, self-imposed or nihilistic) has appeared to have,
at least for the moment, temporarily ended.

Thus, in conclusion, when one speaks on the concept of one's own free will
and volition, it would appear to often stem from a whole wide range of realities
and dynamics (often not aware of it if not receptive, open-minded, self-reflective
or intuitive…) which may include separating 'real life' from 'the illusion,' having
the ability (or thought pattern) to compartmentalize with the desire to 'look forward
to the future' (even idealize); the effort (or 'need and compulsion.' or what Erickson
often refers to as some sort of 'crisis') having the ability to recognize and identify
its existence, and then to engage in its function; the literal, eternal conflict of the
configuration of "the fight or flight syndrome" (whether to instinctively 'fight'
or a kind of futile sense of 'act of avoidance'); one's support system (or lack
there of), or what at times may include a profound lack of self-motivation
(sometimes attributed in psychology to "dysthymia") also due to perhaps
a number of psychological factors such as societal and familial pressures
however accurate or inaccurate (exaggerated or histrionic, more often
than not, stemming from periods of pervasive trauma or the constant
experience and exposure of emotional, spiritual, or psychological abuse);

Some form of depression (situational or chemical) or what one sees
as their potential, perhaps being sullied or contaminated from a form
of subjugation, and this selfsame feeling, emotion, self-image, or outlook
(on existence) from a cognitive-behavioral perspective, becoming hardwired
from a previous experience of an oppressive authority figure, some form of
family dysfunction (which empirically implies a reversal of roles, as well as
often personal, parasitic, and strategic alignments for purposes of power and
control or constant "scapegoating") persistent exposure to the erratic behavior
of one with a severe personality disorder, having the ability (or inability) to
acculturate to the semantics and systems of society's 'shackles' (rituals and
customs) even a government, institution, or psychosocial environment, which
through natural consequences, or other external pressures has squelched one's
desire or 'free will and volition' towards personal successes and achievements,
ambition, self-interest, hope, happiness (ability to dream), growth and development,
once again taking all of these things and dynamics into consideration when considering
the full picture and parameters of its machinations, separating the original dream and
fantasy from the practical, the active-image from the illusion, instinct from intuition, and
a necessary 'state of flux' or constant movement, which often cathartically relieves one from
all those burdens of unnecessary brooding, ruminating, worrying, and perseverating (neuroses).

On The Concept Of Damage -for Charles Bukowski

I have learned that those who do not truly or sincerely know you
(as have been around the block, the city, the country, and world
a couple times) can not do any real damage to you, as long as
you give yourself the proper amount of self-respect and dignity
towards a bit of self-reflection and brooding; that includes all
forms of those so-called scholars, academia, psychologists,
philosophers, even believe it or not, extended family, 'that
neighbor or stranger'…the perfect examples and metaphors
as pathetically and clinically delusional, getting only parsed
'absurd' and wrong distorted information of what they want
to hear to prove their 'gossip and rumor theories' true (of
what they have gotten used to, and even when you start to
do well or resemble some image of what it might mean to
be successful, will go into clinical denial in what it implies
it says about them and will prove every belief or myth and
fable untrue, even a sense of fear and trepidation, touching
on their insecure and fragile identities and egos) because as
the scholar Wilhelm Reich wrote in his infamous manifesto
are just 'little men' and from clinical and behavioral patterns
I have seen and observed, and what I have concluded for the
most part, just have poor 'bedside manner,' insensitive, in-
experienced, fragmented, ('fear of intimacy') maliciously
sarcastic, even mildly sociopathic, while have never ever
really had or experienced in this life and existence anything
close to resembling something of real or true, substantial love
or romance, and in consequence, will always try to, whether
unconscious or conscious (hostile and passive-aggressive)
superimpose that onto you, thus in conclusion, sorry
to break the bad news and sound so scholarly
(short or glib or rude) those who don't know
you can never ever really damage you…

On The Subject Of Surrealism

i am still on-the-run but my dreams getting better
i still love my wife but am still a stranger
i remember as a young runaway
when i used to live way out there
and used to get picked up
by much older women at the
movie theaters way at the end
of the strip malls at the end
of the suburbs with failed
marriages desperately even
delusionally looking to rekindle
something which had been lost
so long ago perhaps some romance
or betrayal or just what life had done
to them and decided on one of those
fine fair and fragrant mornings
to just escape it all and take off
from this new up and coming
business city where they were
putting in paths and promenades
for the pedestrians along the river
putting up a new and exciting rail
system made to resemble old time
streetcars at the turn of the century
putting up lofts and condominiums
(made to look industrial and minimalistic)
for poor rich daughters and their stingy and sleazy
ceo husbands, and we just fled as far as our hearts
would take us like broken-hearted explorers looking
to rediscover the long-lost sacred forgotten foghorn
pacific and not kidding when i tell you at the end
of our journey how many of the mountains just ended
up strangely, primitively, looking like mausoleums of
trees amputated with great big bare mounds of mother
earth of multiple tree stumps like the holy bones of an
excavation plundered and torn asunder, like shattered
chandeliers still hanging from the burntdown decadent
mansions of phantoms, as what else could we really do
at that exact moment but continue to zoom and resume
to our destination, distant, apathetic, almost in a state
of disbelief and denial, like someone who had just witnessed
carnage and their defense-mechanisms instantly go up forced
to compartmentalize for purposes of coping and survival all
the way to the ocean (there's a psychological phenomena

for example where someone experiences a profound
trauma such as molestation or rape and reports
'disassociating' as if it is not even happening to
them while looking down on this whole 'traumatic
event' from another perspective). when we got to the
off-season resorts, which ended up looking more like
some low-lying felliniesque ghost town of vacant motels
and liquor stores and souvenir shops all we could really
do was break down and lay our naked bones in the deserted
dunes and try to make love and fuck it all away i guess serving
a purpose and playing a role for us both, for two lost souls who
had seen better days, disrobed and dazed, a last-ditch, half-crazed
embrace far away from anything that could ever possibly bring pain
blending in with all that's secret and hidden; the resplendent rhythms
of the ocean, which subliminally penetrated our consciousness and
subconsciously marked both the beginning and end; the wild winds
and sins of man and all that remains magically, miraculously swept
up from below; all the sea foam and relics and radiant folklore
tossed up onto shore until some gorgeous little innocent boy
just suddenly showed up out of nowhere retrieving his beach
ball whose facial expression just said it all, looking scared
and shocked, caught completely off guard, picking it up
and scampering back to his mom and at that exact moment
can't begin to tell you nothing could have felt more haunted
and hollow, empty and alone, more of a sense of where had
my life gone; long-gone hero turned to harmless villain
(like some instant keen and sentimental trigger which
separated the past from the present, myth from reality
feeling my senses suddenly explode almost like some
sort of stranded, sci-fi, reverse rebirth at the end of the
world. there is another psychological phenomenon, called
'anadonia' where the individual is incapable of feeling any
sense of pleasure and one wonders if purely chemical
or based as well on a series of traumatic events and
experiences which causes a hardwired and 'numb'
feeling of damage or someone having the compulsive
need usually for past abusive reasons towards some
other sort of self-imposed seclusion) andre breton
the great surrealist french poet once wrote these
brilliant and insightful essays on the subject of
'the surreal' and the proverbial 'theater of the absurd'
probing and wondering where it all comes from; its
images and derivation, and can assure you in my opinion
without even knowing it, a whole heck of a lot of trauma
whether by fate or coincidence; probability and patterns
turning isolated and abandoned, desperate and nihilistic

looking to somehow regenerate and resurrect a whole
new strange postmodern landscape and stark spiritual
metaphysical existence deep-down inside all the way
to the soul already in shambles like watching good old
shakesperian or greek tragedies at one of those dinner
theaters made to look like the coliseum on the outskirts
of the suburbs with your whole instinctive, gluttonous
needs being met, but still strangely feeling a spiritual
neglect, absolutely nothing and vacant, and perversely
triggering a deep-seated, high-expressed emotion of
existential angst which springs up out of nowhere (in
the form of 'racing thoughts' or a mania and hysteria)
vacillating between wondering and worrying, and makes
no tangible sense as alluded to so often by jean-paul sartre.
o yeah? what was it that i was dreaming of last night which
caused me so much to find the need to express myself as
such; my wife and i exploring and experiencing all these
bizarre what we thought to be noble and mythological
paul bunyon characters and their higher-than-holy
hippie girlfriends cutting down the spindles and
spines of great big gorgeous sappy pine forests
to put up another one of those very spare and square
perfect parking lots and lily-white monochromatic malls
as eventually in the long-run was nothing else we could do
in the roar of all their overwhelming 'manifest destiny' chain
saws but to lower our heads and see if we could find our car...

A Didactic List Of Ghosts

1. Ghosts come in many different shapes
and forms when all that grieving and loss
and guilt and conflict and maddening injustice
is just way beyond our control and comprehension

2. They come when it's just too
painful to go back reminiscing

3. They come when they
take over the identity

4. They come in the form of long-lost
visual and auditory hallucinations

5. They come from a hymn and pity and grieving
for the self when all those you thought a part
of your support system suddenly disappear
for no particular reason (most likely the pettiness
and self-interest of human nature) into thin air
which turns thick with spirits wondering where?

6. They come from a severe and profound loneliness
when our coping and survival (and defense) mechanisms
can no longer take it and whether self-inflicted or sudden
trauma or desertion and abandonment is like the scientific
dynamic of the "supersaturation" level where if you drop in
just one more particle everything falls out (and left all alone)

7. They come from very strange and unfamiliar
prolonged periods of weather your physiological
and psychological system is just not prepared for

8. They come from a reel to reel projector
which just keeps on projecting, repeating
your fate over and over and over again

with a very strange form of (in)justice
you cannot even begin to pretend

9. They come from a moodiness
beyond our belief when our hearts
and minds can no longer contain the grief

10. They come from a consistent emotional spiritual
neglect and abuse, leaving one feeling eternally
angry, ruminating, humiliated, and confused

11. They come from the melancholy and mortality
of sentimental seasons in the form of triggers
when our emotional and spiritual and psychological
system just cannot cope or take it anymore and seeps
into the vulnerable fragile folds of an open wounded soul

12. They come from periods and phases of sudden and severe
life-transitions, brooding, isolation, turning inwards, and
depression (whether from trauma, chemical or situational)
and consequently, the real-life hyperbole and personification
and exacerbation of all things empty, hollow, vacant and haunted

13. They come from the skin and bones
of the mind, spirit, heart, and soul…

The Natural Instincts, Configurations,
Choreography And Choruses Of Evolution

One wonders if coyote has an internal clock
when he decides to just step up that slight
mound in the middle of the night and raise
his skull up to the stars and start to howl
like the instant trigger of the salmon when
suddenly decides to just turn around at the
start of winter and take its thousand mile
journey to spawn her eggs down river
like the delivery of ghosts when ghost
stories start to get spoken about them
like the magical symphony of fireflies
and tree frogs after a summer's downpour
like the feening dope addict and petty
thief who really are not that petty at all
like the wife who naturally starts to fill
up the cookie jar because she knows
her man is starting to look good again
and goes through the same customary
routines and rituals of staking her claim
like when soulmate or lover through solitary
pain, loss, and suffering knows the exact time
her man is turning around and returning home
from his necessary, nihilistic, bold, fateful journey
like the industrious beaver at the entrance
of the lagoon who diligently digs and
builds his domicile twig by twig by
twig by twig and just as contented in
the preparation and construction of it
like those nocturnal creatures of the swamp
who start to sound like a seesaw of old splintered
rocking chairs right when the dusk turns to night
like the secret raid of rabbits going after the bulbs
after the soul after the gold like slick sleepwalkers
like stalkers stealing roses from the tombstones
like the moon rising over the mountain somehow in
the exact same spot making you feel alive once more
like the pretty young lady in the big city during long
dreary days of winter all bundled up in layers of bleak
clothing and when the spring strangely suddenly shows
up around the corner, starts to take it off, turning every
'mild-mannered man' into madman into prey from her
seductions with her natural need and compulsion
to shed, strip off, and reveal parts of her body

one wonders if the coyote has an internal clock when he
decides to just step up that slight mound in the middle
of the night and raise his skull to the stars and howl?

Cops & Robbers (and the healing power of snow)

Can it also snow on the moon and do they get a day off from school?
I remember one of those days when it was really building up beautiful
in one of those parks in The Lower East Side where we all used to hang
out when we had nothing better to do with our lives during a period of time
when the police weren't getting along too well with the residents and there
was a fine line between who was really starting or committing the crime
and suddenly before you knew it just like that for the fun of it some kid
decided to just fling a snowball right at a cop of which of course they
instantly returned fire until all you saw were all these silhouetted snowballs
being hurled back and forth across the sky in the middle of that wild snowfall
both sides out of control, blissful, hysterical, cracking-up between the young
cops and delinquents and even a policeman innocently exclaiming–"I really
 needed this!" which instantly seemed to break up and heal all the friction
and tension and relieve a little bit all the stigmatization and it was scenes
or moments like this looking back almost makes you want to break
down and cry, while it is of my sincerest belief for those who have
spent a good and decent amount of time in the big city with the
snow slashing past the muffled streetlights and lamplights how
much prettier and holier and quiet, transcendent, sacred, and
silent allowing you some real downtime for spiritual recovery
and reflection, even healing and redemption about humanity
and the madness of life down some long-lost lovely pristine
eternal blanket of ethereal snow with no borders which just
seemed to flow on forever that everything might just be alright.

Right Around That Nightclub Adam's Apple

I remember *Bagel Nosh* sitting in the window
of that gigantic bagel in uptown Manhattan
with eyes bloodshot at 3 in the morning
with burnout buddies having discovered
their divorced mother's stash conveniently
stashed in her night table rolling up the joints
with the seeds and sticks still in them when
all night nude cable and midget wrestling was
still big looking out towards The United Nations
brooding beat ragged disheveled void and vacant as
that to me was true diversity, existential, intellectualism

Those experiences expanding your horizons like your
eyes opening with the sun coming up over the mountain.

One Of Those Moods

1

All man needs is a pail pale peach wooden shack
with banana tree in back and shutters to welcome
in and shut out seasons and invisible chameleon
constantly wheezing and woman he dreams
of back east in the good part of The Bronx

2

Too many cities and states I've taken off from
in the middle of the night right around dawn
and swear can recall every solitary motel
room and sidewalk and each had their own
miraculous revelation of a scent of reborn in
the bleary-eyed morning (somewhere between
the pine needle wilderness mist and steam
sweeping in from the corner) from Oregon
to Washington to Reno to San Francisco
and San Francisco once more Butte
Cheyenne Denver and New Orleans
and New Orleans too many times
before wrestling with the law and
lord and man god I've paid my
dues and treasured each one

3

Burned-out parts of the city
I always declared my love for
them with boys howling in alley
a pink mandolin in the pharmacy
window, the old Puerto Rican men
playing dominoes on the sweltering
midnight corner and picking up plantain
and *Coronas*, bleary-eyed in blaring bodegas
finally pleased and contented to be anonymous
alone and not a single soul knowing me except
that much younger girl trying to make her mine
still living with her mom from the madness of my little
corner of strange ultra-orthodox Cloisters to The Bronx

4

Once you're perfectly responsible
might as well be one of those
idiot slave husbands might
as well be one of those dead
ducks hanging backwards from
its ankles in an alcove in China
town but goes down so well
with Vietnamese coffee

5

The Asian boys
slap handball
passionately
with mad heart
and soul against
the wall trying to impress
their girls in the pale purple
dusk before the sun falls
and turns the marquee
a powder-blue which
reads *Pioneer Hotel*

This is where strangers
come to die be reborn
and die once more...

6

Murder, mayhem and mermaids
discovered in a fishnet, fluttering
with their dreams ripped from them

7

The parrot breaks out his cage
and becomes his own man and
interestingly is resented for wanting
to seek his independence and develop
his own identity not placed upon him

8

Why should he have to wait for those boys
from the dead end who murder cats
and hurl stones at poor dogs
behind invisible fences

9

Dostoevsky getting thrown out of
the walk-in clinic, literally thrown out
and we see him flying out the window
sprung backwards in his rags and long beard
eyes bugged-out even farcical; the ambulances
showing up shuttling him in the back heading
out towards Hospital Hill where they keep the local
Walmart, pet shop,.motels and boxcar diner; taking
down a Christmas tree farm to put up a psychiatric hospital.
Out here, they don't really allow you to express your opinion
even though the nurses were so mechanical and mean-spirited
and all he really needed was just a little Otis Redding tenderness.
They get stuck in bumpadabumpa traffic of a funeral procession
giving them a little downtime to drop him in a burlap bag for his
own personal solitary confinement for his crime and punishment

10

Nodding-out to Chet Baker in my rowboat
flowing down the rapids sea why he turned
off and turned on as the advantages far outweigh
anything in this pathetic silly reality going into my
7th hour of trying to apply for some position to get
a pittance to get a password and still haven't gotten it
Kafkaesquely going back & forth to William Burroughs
doldrums sending you round and round in circles just to
transport Alzheimer's patients through the high mountains
ironically causing you to lose your mind and patience
nodding-out in my wrinkled linen hand-me-down suit
of late-autumn heading towards the lost and eternal
lagoon of true-blue splendor and magnificence

11

I've considered swapping dreamcatcher crucifix
which hangs over bed for Batman & Robin
to fight off the crimes of existence

12

The gravesite by the gravesite
by the gravesite by the gravesite
not too far from that babbling river
which runs under the bridge towards
The Dairy Cream whose opening and re
birth a bit late due to the delayed Spring

13

One should eventually die in a town and city
they have love and respect for and then can
at least claim they "made it" in one form
or another. When I used to work those slave
hours at that mental health clinic that phony
hypocritical supervisor who no one could stand
for the exact selfsame reason used to make these
bullshit suggestions at the treatment plan meetings
(as this is what sounded like the right crunchy thing
to do but was so damn patronizing and never took
you seriously) that we should offer anonymous
suggestions to boost team morale, and thought
it wouldn't be a bad idea to have our own softball
team to compete against the other mental health
clinics in that depressed part of New England, but
then thought what the fuck, I'd now have to devote
my weekends in spending more time with phony-baloney
schmucks I couldn't stand or have anything in common
who abuse power or for that matter never return phone
calls (in the mental health field mind you) like that
annual luncheon at the CEO's country club I would
always skip out on, like what, should feel honored
to be there and sit around those caddy gossiping
tables giving out plaques and awards to the same
schmuck supervisors as would shock you if I told
you what was talked about behind closed doors
and my god if you talk about confidentiality and

a supposed code of ethics in a field whose core
principles and values are based on the foundation
to restore one's dignity, trust, and self-respect?

Interesting, I kept on getting clients based on
recommendations for the good and hard work
I was doing with these kids, but never uttered
a damn thing at one of these events, as just felt
like people talking way too loud (about themselves)
who falsely represented, and never got closure over
most vital stages of human growth and development

14

In my days of youth looking back at such cliches and expressions
when they'd make such obvious sweeping generalizations like he's
just 'calling-out for help' I remember thinking what the fuck does that
mean and what does that even look like calling-out for help looking
at the hypocrisies of these higher-than-holy adults and sexually-
repressed assholes like you're the exact reason why I'm stealing
and can't stay out of trouble and if in fact this were true and you've
supposedly identified all the traits and symptoms with your quick
clinical conclusions how come you're doing absolutely nothing?

15

People ask me how I spent my early
adulthood and I tell them scouring
through The NY Times trying to find
a good and decent and fine unknown
foreign film and getting the times that
part from that part from that part from
that part never mattered so much how
it ended or even for that mattered how
it started because in those films it was
all about characters and left wondering
what happened and always ended some
where right in the middle like that old man
returning home with his fish all wrapped up in
newsprint not really caring about the headlines

16

When Florida used to just be a glossy postcard
which read "Paradise" and a fresh new pair
of white leather *Pumas* with a sky-blue
stripe which rode right down the middle

17

When I redeem myself and get rich again
am gonna get my winter home in Brighton
Beach, Brooklyn and my summer home in
Riverdale or The Cloisters section. When we
used to go on vacation to places like Antigua
they'd have these little signs stuck to the back
of the door in *The Holiday Inn* said something
like if you get caught smoking marijuana would
be severely prosecuted and held to the strictest
punishment and thought yeah I'm gonna spend
the rest of my life in an Antiguan prison never
crossed my consciousness like eating lemon
Hostess Pies on the corner of *7-11* when the
trains came rattling in at rush hour knowing
Ishould be home doing my homework

18

When in Rome...
never really
understood
bullshit like
that as always
found myself
nodding-out
on dope in
brown suit
right off
the rack
from Penn
Station to
Hoboken
walking
it off in
midnight

windy
cobble
stone

19

Your wife like one of those perfect meat timers
who pops out of that gorgeous succulent duck
and I'm like that portly man who's just gotten
beaten from way too much living and have
to bury in the strings of his Baby Grande

20

You start to gradually awake again
like an old beaten man with purpose
diligently pushing his shopping cart
with a simple case of *Miller Beer* at
Walmart when you hear Billie Holiday
I mean Buddy Holly's first old time
rock & roll yodeling from Lubbock
Texas through the speakers up here
in the high mountains of Montpelier

21

A jigsaw puzzle piece
falls off a globe
of the world.

Somewhere Right Around Then

I think the reasons for my depression is all my dreams and wishes
have come true and not even aware of it or much deeper on a more
shallow level or vice-versa like that great big mug right by the side
of my bed with the leftover residue of hot chocolate beaujolais
and blood or maybe just miss the rain of harlem. my sister went
to barnard. she was three years older. and remember her inviting me
to some party of hers and all her friends being pretty impressed and
felt just as smart or at least as well read especially with my buzz from
the blunts or getting drunk on red red wine the hit of the day by that rock
& roll reggae-influenced white band from england and suddenly her close
friend harry lipman asking me if i wanted to toss frisbee and simply flinging
that free-floating disk the length of the quad in the middle of the deep dark
night hollering out loud spotting and catching it right before it was about
to hit our heads and looking back at that image with all that spontaneity
and adrenaline and at last living for the moment felt like the pure perfect
blissful beautiful parable of reality then all suddenly hailed and hopped
into a taxi flying down broadway towards studio 54 with the late spring
windows rolled down and me yelling something cracking-up silly sincerely
hysterical like—"hey harry's got the frisbee!" and had it very poignantly
pressed to his palm with the centrifugal force from the mad and wild
breeze keeping it up and there we all were all drunk passed-out alive
dead to the world and harry very focused with this proud casual smile
balancing a frisbee against the palm of his hand barreling down broadway
while this spare zen image seemed to sum it all up and when we got there
we all fell out of the cab harry subtly secretively tucking that frisbee beneath
his pants like some sort of lifelong companion or slapstick gun he always kept
with him and we all got in wasted thinking my sister might actually be on ecstasy
the new drug of the day dancing half-crazed all over the place may be the last really
good memory i had but can't be think it was like 1982, 83, may have even been 1984.

Joseph D. Reich

Time Warped

Staggering home from keg parties
   felt like a whole other lifetime ago
       in many ways it was
         in many ways it wasn't
through the foreign familiar streets
    of the suburbs
  knowing exactly
     where you were
       with no direction
         drunken, disoriented
the closest you would
    ever get to home
      & when you got home
        (still somehow
         felt so far away from home)
  finishing off some novel
     speed-reading
      stream of consciousness
        by some big window
         with a brook overflowing
  while looking back
    the teacher ironically
      absurdly
     would ask you
       about mood & theme & environment
and thought about it
always being autumn
always felt very lonely
    wishing they could grade you
   on intuition
on your shattered soul
   like some long-lost lanternman
  nodding-out
somewhere
   between
     the night & dawn
      eternally
       at a loss for words
waking up on the weekend
in the bleak morn late noon
of high school with a hangover
    having blacked-out
      not remembering
        a thing you did

                              the night before
while reflecting back at your existence
            felt like this very much
                    was the prime of your life
                              & the grand metaphor.

Joseph D. Reich

Psych!

i think when i grew up i had all this trepidation and anxiety
and worrying because knew i could never live up to or more
so these were the people i was supposed to live up to while
deep down shallow in my subconscious just knew that they
weren't worth it so just started to act-out without being aware
of it and stealing right and left becoming something of a thief-
comedian taking from those figures of authority (who had taken
from me) even kiss asses i wasn't particularly impressed with
who i believed to be phony and full of shit and really lacked integrity
and had a whole grocery list of things i had proudly recklessly taken
to prove it but interestingly experienced the perverse psychological
phenomenon while numb of only feeling pleasure with those things
i had stolen yet had a whole other facet of my personality where
i used to love to do extra reading so i might have another tool in
my arsenal and they could never get anything over on me and turned
towards the russians like dostoevsky the beatniks the french symbolists
such as baudelaire and rimbaud and much later on jean genet who couldn't
keep himself out of trouble and prison (loved the story how jean-paul sartre
used to bail him out cause he saw something in him that he just couldn't see
in himself and knew had something worthy to offer) of course just like every
other kid where i was from was mandated to see a psychiatrist while ironically
all the connections came from other similar ridiculous driven-like parents who
were workaholics also neglecting their kids and often used to think when i'd read
those bumper stickers during all that bumpa'da'bumpa didn't really care or even
felt resentful they'd still have to preach and remind us jesus died for us although
seemed like a pretty decent guy and also quite fond of as well that dude during
vaudeville times who used to just secretly stand right off stage with that great
gigantic hook (how do you get a job like that?) and pull all the schnucks away.

Rolling Dice In The Bones Of Paradise

Miserable doctors stuffed in the elevator of the hospital
with the pigment of newsprint and duel diagnoses of
Napoleonic Complex and clinical Narcissism, and
because of their criteria and obsessive-compulsive
symptoms, their wives constantly leave them
engaged in a very strange ritual and obnoxious
power-struggle and hierarchy where they don't even
make eye contact but very mechanically, meticulously
like some passive-aggressive, higher-than-holy form
of interrogation, punitively scrutinize the identity tag
of their fellow colleagues where the brain surgeon
sneers at the family physician who sneers at the
pediatrician who sneers at the physician assistant
who sneers at the x-ray technician until they all
end up questioning each other, and when they
leave, questioning themselves. New wings keep
on getting added and donated by philanthropists
of old money with hx's of chemical-dependency
problems and first born sons of self-fulfilling
prophecies, constantly in trouble with the law
getting bailed out by the family lawyer "brought
up" on gun charges. The campus is composed
of a manicured forest with tame coyotes and
trained boars and wealthy daughters who were
able to afford good colleges, and through the
passed-down custom of nepotism from generation
to generation can get any job they want and wander
around with that debutante sense of self-importance,
privilege and entitlement, like the whole world revolves
around them. Security always puts on that idiot act
of suspicion but have absolutely no street smarts or
instincts and always end up harassing and attaching
a stigma to the gentle giant minding his own business
checked on by young and innocent and sympathetic
nurses straight from the farm looking for someone
to take care of them and become their father-figure
because their boyfriends are abusive and treat them
like second-class citizens. Female clowns nod-out
in the elevator with flamboyant, resentful, paranoid
pastors. The most contented seems to be the chef
in the cafeteria with that comically lopsided bent
over hat behind steaming dishes of meatloaf and
mash potatoes and prides himself in having an affair
with the secretary in Renal. Sitting smack-dab all alone

right in the middle of one of those long spacious halls
decked-out in windows (which brings in the beautiful
melancholic madness of the seasons) like some sort of
museum exhibit is a splendid grand piano with gold ropes
all around it, and whether by coincidence or not, always an
empty spot, which leaves room for the imagination; for ghost
spirits of past lovers and acquaintances, and perversely through
this obscure emptiness, makes you feel more safe and secure
in this thing they like to call and refer to as your time on earth.

1969, Los Angeles

It all seemed to stem from that simple spare image
and never knew why he was so obsessed with it...
of Benjamin Braddock played by Dustin Hoffman
in "The Graduate" in his red Alfa Romeo flying
over The Golden Gate Bridge to the soundtrack
by Simon & Garfunkel specifically written for this
(as originally swear the lyrics were supposed to be
'here's to you Mrs. Rockefeller') after Mrs. Robinson's
shenanigans having had fallen in love with her gorgeous
innocent daughter as that there in that exact moment
was where lied all those lies and betrayals; how he
had been set up and framed and misinterpreted
and underestimated just seemed to sum it all up
and say it all about the phony hypocritical bullshit
overbearing adult grownup world; of course as well
there was that image when the only place he could
escape his loud obnoxious father and his colleagues
at the pool party thrown for him and didn't feel a part
of it in the scuba outfit he had purchased him and just
sloshed over in all his armor through all their muted hollering
and leaped beneath to the bottom of the deep blue pool only
place which seemed he could vanish to just sitting there
blowing bubbles brooding with his harpoon while similarly
at the end when he couldn't quite get to the church on time
to rescue her and him (like some sadistic little trick of Mrs.
Robinson's) she hollered out loud in her virgin-white wedding
dress as if suddenly recognizing and coming back to life declaring
her mutual love and they both took off through that awful flock of
grownups beating them off with a cross and then locking them down
in the church with that crucifix and fleeing once again and catching
up to that commuter bus suddenly showing up out of nowhere taking
off to the happily ever after horizon both sitting in the back holy
and hysterical thoughtful and introspective far more humane
and human than any one of them to the lost unpredictable
unknown remote future and now much older it was all
crystal clear to him understanding and getting it all.

Joseph D. Reich

Phoenix

i wonder how that old facebook friend of mine is doing? she was this pretty nice single mother with a son from arizona, who i think was an art teacher and every time she'd get mad or frustrated for good reason would literally go right out into her yard and punch a cactus, and really admired her for that, but then in the long-run, eventually like everything else would end up feeling guilty for losing her temper. she used to tell me how in the morning when ever she went jogging through the desert how these really sleazy guys would say lewd shit to her through the window of their pickups, and would express it over facebook and diss them and for good reason the whole male gender hoping i think that they'd somehow figure out who she was talking about. she said when she was a little girl whenever she'd get into a fight with her mother she'd slip out her bedroom window in tears and disappear similarly into the desert evening. i wonder what she is doing now as seemed to vanish just like everything else while likewise when we moved up here to the mountaintops of vermont my facebook page just froze up but they probably would't have ended up showing up to my funeral anyway because they never ever seemed to ask questions and only spoke about themselves and complained.

For Gregory Corso & Holden Caufield

Sometimes when my wife turns indifferent towards me it is maddening
and drives me crazy cuz i know i've always been there for her through
thick and thin and don't know what i've done to deserve this (and think
that's the whole existential point of it; i've done nothing to deserve it
and maybe it's just got nothing to do with this and sometimes i think
just a difference between the sexes) as know i've been supportive of
her through every situation or crisis whether big or small so not so
much the substance but the hypocrisy of it all, yet when i do my
nightly sleepwalk through the halls and wake up to the light of
the refrigerator and see all the things that she's done for me
and my son, i can't help but to instantly, insanely love her
again. it's a really fucked-up and strange thing. last night
during one of my episodes i dreamed i believed i saw those
scenes of *midnight cowboy* they didn't show the public and
showed ratso rizzo and joe buck, two fugitives on-the-run
with this really good looking young gorgeous country girl
pulling off her sundress and making love to her separately,
as she was naturally willing and kept on waiting for when
they would enter the city but they never made it nor did i,
and finally the sheriff and townsmen caught up with them
and they dug and burrowed a tunnel beneath their motel
room and the whole posse sent in the dogs even different
sorts of animals and the sheriff, a stray cub, and then i
woke up but was relieved that they seemed to get away.
i don't know sometimes i think it was just easier when i
lived alone in brooklyn and remember that morning on the
platform of the subway reading in the headlines of the paper
how they had shot and killed tupac shakur and that really
took me back some. i'm not so sure about this thing called
marriage as appears at times to be a constant petty and trivial
impossible futile power-struggle. maybe that's why they call it
"the institution" (or as chris rock cleverly and comically argues
how nelson mandella survived all those years of torture in prison
but couldn't get with it after he got out and he and his wife got
divorced just six months later) as literally just dawned on me
maybe that's why ratso rizzo and joe buck just suddenly showed
up in my dream, two fugitives on-the-run naturally having sex with
that gorgeous young country girl, but what'ya gonna do? and recently
ironically been looking for rooms right there out there on the strip in vegas.

A Strange Way Of Looking At Things

i have decided when i finally
      go i want to be one of those
            ole time nostalgic hong kong
                        pu-pu platters
    showing up
       all lit on fire
           in a nice dim chinese restaurant
with fresh clean tablecloths
        & a polite family
            with good table manners
   not all fucked-up & dysfunctional
        & share & distribute me
             equally & when they are
all good & done & ceremonially stuffed
        put some of those warm
              steaming towels
                  over their mugs
             to sob into
       & contemplate the history
           of the world stuffing those
               different color flavored mints
                   into their corduroy pockets
                              to save for later.

Price Chopper

In this part of town they drive through with refrigerators,
bales of hay, and wild roosters with signs which read
such things like on medical buildings–"Please do
not bring firearms or your dangerous weapons in"
with a panoramic sweeping view of the mountains
right across from the granite mines; you ironically
see inside The Price Chopper this old timer with
a pirate patch on and something of a long dagger
all buttoned-up in a sheath attached to his hip
I guess in case he might end up needing it in
the wine or frozen food section; you head back
home past that town diner where they religiously
serve literal blue plate specials made up of meatloaf
and mash potatoes, those little awful dishes of peas
and carrots yet the parking lot is always packed and
does better business than Disneyland as I guess it is all
about location and being family-owned and who you know
go past that medical center again with this old Charlie
Chaplin character patiently waiting with his cane for
his wife to pick him up and when she does he just
naturally swaggers out like a humble obedient kind
old dog, like that slapstick comedian; slide, shuffle,
slide off to the horizon; similarly when you get home,
you will calm yourself and chill out to a cheap jug of
sparkling supermarket wine straight from The Sonoma
Valley with the weather muted just like you like it
to check out different parts of The Continental U.S.
to someone who calls himself Dr. Philadelphia and
that seductress in her tight-fitting blue dress which
highlights all her contours and body parts like Freud's
madonna whore mistress who might just actually even
bring me leftovers while isn't that all we ever asked for?

Joseph D. Reich

On The Nature Of Weather (sci-fi vs. suicide)

After they cut down all the trees and forest
and cut the ceremonial ribbon and put up
neat and tidy rows of climate-controlled
condominiums which used to look out
to farmland and ocean now right around
the corner from the tinted medical and
business parks where you can't look
in but they can look out right around
the corner where they all got pleasantly
uprooted and transferred and moved
families with views of perfect cookie-
cutter manicured monochromatic
strip malls and promenades
which were all made to
resemble everyday
happily-ever-after
life and existence
with enough space
and emptiness to feed
the swans and go jogging
and 'simple and easy access
to shopping and the highway'
yet somehow things just don't
seem quite right these people
or what they like to refer to as
residents and commuters don't
seem exactly all there and feel
just as distant and faceless
and expressionless as these
imitative fit-to-form made-to-
resemble real-life structures
of faux scenarios and dream
of taking one of those farm-
o-psuedo-calls perhaps
a couple maybe even half
a bottle to get you out of
here any way possible.

4 Reasons To Become An Expatriate

1.

i don't know why they can't just make the superbowl like at some decent
hour, like the rest of the sporting events in america, as seems like they're
just trying to stretch it out as long as possible, like some orgasm from a girl
you have no true feelings for, making space for all those gimmick commercials
with their punch lines, which never seem to pay off in the long-run, 'cause trying
way too hard, nonstop commenting by those you have no respect for and whole
tables chock-full of sportscasters like some jesus' last supper where you just
wish they were all taken out and murdered and the only soul survivor jesus

2.

christ all sponsored by doritoes and guacamole and budweiser or maybe
just be like one of those great big art exhibitions with all that hype which
can't help but to be anti-climactic, and thus all this anxiety and uptight
all filled up with pseudo-intellects and aristocrats and art critics, while
the real true-blue starving artist just prefers to be left the hell alone
(playing hide & go seek) in the coat closet, making small talk and
gets so much more out of the cute 16 year old hat check girl

3.

i want to plant my perennial garden like one of those exotic gardens
in some desert out in tunisia, maybe even sprinkle it or pepper it with
the poppy for one of those long-lost lethargic warm days on the patio
contemplating along with some palm wine fresh dates and lemon tea
bread when simply just got nothing left to do and nothing left to say

4.

these days having a hard time making the distinction
between my dreams and nightmares, but at least in
those bad dreams, able to get full closure over those
past phony friends weren't particularly sincere or loyal.

Joseph D. Reich

A Brunch For Strangers

a warm breeze rippling off the lake clattering the colored glass
spheres in the maples fluttering through the screen window
to the hanging house plants and books on the coffee table

your arms the back of your neck your ribcage always shivering
when taking those foreign ferries through the mediterannean
but those memories somehow sentimentally last forever

you remember when they put up those first lofts in
soho over the cobblestone in the early-seventies
breakfast always tasted better with a hangover.

Making A Self For Your Name

I.

'so much depends'
on *the clash*...
by a whole mess
of white chickens
being sent back
a day early from
europe for stealing
returning home
humiliated sulking
'neath my leather
ten-gallon i picked
up in monmartre...

revolution some
       thing they can
never steal from
           you

II.

a perfect sized pumpkin
looking as if it's fallen
from the heavens
onto a leftover
keg of beer

looking back at existence
everything appeared like
something of a phase
or life-transition

III.

how did that carol king
song go again? –"i feel the earth
move under my feet, i feel the sky
tumbling down, a tumbling down…"

For William Carlos Williams Physician From Patterson

The camera takes a close-up of the perfect right breast of the cheerleader
in her tight red pullover sweater and a glistening pasted-on *Dentyne* million
dollar smile in Madison, Wisconsin in the land of milk and honey, while
the rich bratty privileged and entitled boys and girls from the fraternities and
sororities will get all the opportunities. The rest of the student body pretend
to be all hostile and scary in front of the tv cameras from those o so rough
and tough safe and secure silver spoon suburbs. The veteran referee with
a heart of gold will limp home for another shot of cortisone, while the idiot
balding middle-aged coaches with their coats off will engage in meltdowns
and temper-tantrums, as they represent their colleges and conferences
and get paid by the alumni and boosters who want to see conviction and
winning records. The real true-blue heroes from the inner city and ghetto
if they don't make it to the pros will never get a fighting chance. After
waking up from nodding-out in your easy chair you swear it says on
the tickertape below–'Chris Paul out for 6 weeks due to orthoscopic
surgery on a figment of his imagination.' You stagger bleary-eyed down
the hall to turn off your son's nightlight making it tradition to fall asleep
with a book fallen to the floor all curled up with his wild wavy curls having
lovely innocent dreams and the only thing you really ever find worth living for.

Just Like Chuck Norris & Christey Brinkley

After a night of insomnia
you watch the 3 stooges
the best thing to watch
after a night of insomnia
then it naturally goes into
an infomercial on identity
theft and will stop identity
theft or restore the identity
that you no longer got left
or after getting your identity
back will monitor your identity
and thinking why do i want all
these strangers i don't even
know in some random office
now monitoring my identity
and doesn't make me feel
any more safe or secure
but in fact feel more insecure
and show all the young status-
quo i guess what the young status-
quo do these days which is just
sit around all day at cafes with
that what 'ya call very important
and necessary wifi and will even
monitor your identity there when
you're sitting down there all day
at the cafe and i'm also thinking
why are you even going out to a
cafe if you're gonna just be sitting
there all day looking down at your
screen but that's ironically 'neither
here nor there' as didn't it used to
just be about "people watching" or
trying to meet somebody and then
by the end of the infomercial having
to do with identity theft which seems
to literally and existentially have been
stolen a long time ago suddenly feeling
all safe and secure and zen and at one
with the universe and world while this very
neat and tidy responsible prudent woman
in her very neat and tidy office perfectly
contented living happily ever after types
at her computer and they show her even

with that extra tv offer of a free shredder
at a $20 value and with a convenient grin
on in the comforts of her home shredding
some paper as this image will 'guarantee
and bring full satisfaction' and bring her
closer to the heart and soul of her identity
and decide instead rather to look out my
window at the new gorgeous miraculous
accumulation of snow we got during my
night of insomnia with ethereal branches
of pine being weighed down to the ground
blissfully hiding our picnic table and after
waking up from my easy chair during these
iridescent snowfalls always have some of
the most warm and sexy dreams which in
my opinion has so much more to do with the
true kind and compassionate core of identity.

The Loneliest Man In The World

i always had this macabre dream
of living in this very long thin room
in new york city they refer to as
railroad apartments or for short
railroads right over the flickering
spinning tickertape of central park
way atop of columbus circle and
live & die a happy man in the deep
opaque safe shadows of the beaming
red hue of the letters and numbers of
world news and never be lonely again
knowing that throbbing bleak light
of tragedy of scores of soaring
degrees of sudden plummeting
stocks is constantly permeating
right through the fragile anatomy
of my poor broken bones & am
finally at one with the solitary
starving stoned rhythms of man.

Yeshiva

I remember working that whole steamy summer
in the murray hill section of manhattan right near
grand central station graveyard shift behind
the front desk of this fancy-schmanzy hotel
with that older guy whose wife had just left
him and went lesbian, and myself as well
coming off a bad relationship, looking back
whether subconscious, cathartic, or just trying
somehow to work through it every time we had
a conflict, i'd insist taking after the late-great
inspector cluseau–"the problem is sol-ved!"
and he would instantly snap back very literal
and hostile–"the problem is *not* sol-ved!"
and in retrospect how this exchange was
so humorous as these exact semantics
even ironic and would try to escape
the desk every chance i could checking
the halls and helping miserable middle-
aged women out with their neurotic issues

I eventually got in much better shape and found
someone far younger and prettier even getting that
borderline woman back a little and marrying this good
looking girl from the bronx my second year of internship.

No Translation

They all got blown away in that bar
        in that smoky pool hall in sleepy hollow
                              that night
                                    of believe it or not karaoking
                as everything had grinded
                        to a sudden halt
                              those moments of slow-motion
                                      of emotional loss
                        lost & found & lost once more
                  his girlfriend stunned
        as if belting one directly to the gods
   never knew he had had it in him
& where it came from
      like discovering some long-lost psalm
             from some martyr on his deathbed
                     who had been silenced
            & abandoned & alienated
    his whole existence
misinterpreted
  by the wrong people
     by the mobs & the masses
            & was the real hero
                & saved them
                      singing the refrain
              to that gorgeous meatloaf song–
"i want you, i need you, but there ain't no way i'm ever gonna love you"
                       & was the first time
                            when they had shuffled home
                      through the shadows
                in the deep darkness
           right before the dawn
    where they all just shut the fuck up
& there was absolutely no small talk
              but pure reflection & silence
                    & could hear everything thawing
         in the miraculous mellifluous season
the pell-mell melt-off of snow
    flowing through the gutters
        the flapping of nightbirds
              even the river
           & that chorus of radiant
                redemptive foghorns
                     & knew after that performance
                awestruck

Joseph D. Reich

                              at a loss for words
                        which had moved everyone to tears
     nothing would ever be the same again.

That Song "Landslide"

He had forgotten to forget...

Now sits back in the constellations
gazing down to the planet earth

His new addiction good ole Stevie Nicks...

That radiant rich raspy voice of hers which just kept on seeming
to get better and better, deeper and more distinguished with
age, closer to the ragged and raging broken heart and soul.

He wondered if he would really call this an addiction but not more
so something of an instinctive and primal feening and appreciation
after all the bullshit of how life and existence breaks you down and spits
you out and now a necessary sublimation of the senses and sight and sound

Even those brilliant lovely love ballads she had done with Tom Petty
and Don Henley, especially recently for some reason the song "Landslide"
which just made him break down and cry every time he heard her lyrics
with Lindsey Buckingham, her past boyfriend and flame just standing
there solitary, sentimentally at center stage plucking the pure melody.

He and his wife right after they got married went to Fleetwood Mac's
reunion concert through all that mad summer traffic from Providence
Rhode Island all the way out to Atlantic City and seemed like something
of a worthy juggernaut of bumpadabumpa cars to try and weave and wind
in and out all the way at the end of some long-lost burnt-out shot boardwalk.

Of course they stayed at a beat down bedbug motel with a brilliant
postmodern apocalyptic view of the projects and casinos at dusk
and felt something like a classic old Bruce Springsteen song
or at least the first couple of albums when he was passionate
and poverty-stricken and poor and had nothing else to live for

and when they took off at sundown and finally found parking
found a whole lot of bummed-out geriatrics, zombied-out in
smoky rows in front of old slot machines just pulling the levers
back and forth like automatons under the influence of mixed
drinks and buzzers and beepers, like some Starship Fleet
futilely fighting and heading towards some shattered galaxy

and knew at that exact moment why he had decided to get
married or at least what he told his friends and acquaintances
and fellow peers at Wurzweiler School of Social Work and that

Joseph D. Reich

if he was gonna spend and go through the rest of this life being eternally lonely
why not do it with somebody he sincerely loved or might make him happy…

Turned out Stevie and Lindsey were so on point and alive that night
emotional and sentimental and even holy and heartfelt, and their
reunion concert felt almost like getting back together again after
some long and rough heartbreaking breakup, and that the seediness
and sadness of it all was well worth it; got a fine sleep in that beat down
motel on the outskirts and guess was able to look a little forward to the future.

Bittersweet Aphorisms Of The Seasons: With
Your Own Free Additional Guide For Survival

"Well the night does funny things inside a man
These ol' tomcat feelings you don't understand"

>   -Tom Waits

~

What was the subconscious before it became conscious
as believe at times better left alone like a language
which betrays itself by those not always so well in-
tended leaving one confused, lost, empty, and alone

~

The things that kill you are the things that you try not to think about
and all that doubt in the constant fluctuating soft hard core of denial

~

One wonders what phobias and superstitions were before they existed
and does not that image take on something of a Zen-Buddhist quality?

~

Freedom is having the ability to dream about the future

~

Keen, those profound 'high-expressed' feelings
of childhood and youth when you dreamed
of your future, who would ever 'imagine'
it was then which held the most presence?

~

During puberty we were all freaks in the way (and ways)
we chose to process (or not process) and distort things

~

Whenever I heard some girl liked me I always experienced
this instant sensation and feeling of a strange violation
and it was only when I got older when circumstances and
situations got desperate that I was able to return the favor

~

Imagine lying in the bare naked belly
of the girl you had your first wet dream
to and meet up coincidentally like thirty
years later whispering sweet nothings
and pillow talk realizing it's all one big
illusion and how you survived and coped
and take off with the exact same bicycle
through the tender dewdrop branches
of the strange silent suburb at dawn
and realize absolutely nothing's
changed at all really just
the mood you're in and
need someone to take
care of you to the end

~

Nightmares and dreams ping-pong
between fantasy and reality where
the subconscious is a sibling rivalry
sometimes good sometimes bad
and your mortality a referee
not sure whose side he's on

~

Masturbation is the best reenactment
of something kind and compassionate
an instant escapism and liberation leading
to a lucid clarity and redemption in the moment

~

Pillow talk is promises you mean to keep which have been broken

~

To me looking back at my life it's all those who were
not quite exactly honest who I saw as the biggest liars

~

There's another one of those brilliant expressions
'to be brutally honest,' which appears accurate
but also sounds the exact opposite, and seems
to have developed this derivation and trait and
characteristic from the suffering (of the dishonest)
and constantly stigmatized and demonized and
underestimated and misinterpreted, and eventually
'getting through it' to become the declarative statement
and proclamation of what it means to be brutally honest

~

Why does it consistently appear we paradoxically
always try to live up to those standards of those
who have absolutely no real standards (often blatant
hypocrisies and contradictions) and a baseline (of
integrity and compassion) so below us, shallow and
superficial, who really couldn't give a damn coming
from that infamous breed of 'damned if you damned
if you don't,' while clinically, cognitively hardwired
going back to that vacillating, vicious abuse cycle
from where all the trauma originally began, as
psychologically and spiritually so overwhelming
and beyond the realm of our understanding and
comprehension, literally develop a self-image of
such self loathing, end up 'taking it out on ourselves'
becoming self-destructive, fulfilling the self-fulfilling prophecy

Joseph D. Reich

~

Those who deliberately make others feel guilty
is something of a 'petty crime' and miss/demean/or...
Just deconstruct that sentence and consider the phonetics
and sound of that statement (pun intended) making one feel
'guilty,' while thereafter, consequently, those who play possum
and come up with such obvious and predictable, cookie-cutter,
hackneyed declarations like–'only you can make yourself feel
guilty' are ironically far more guilty of a serious crime, like after
a crime has already been committed and consciously showing absolutely
no remorse or contrition, gross and vulgar, deliberately manipulative,
dehumanizing and belittling, making that person feel like they don't
even exist (that of the existential 'stranger') having stripped them
of all human characteristics, self-image, self-motivation, and spirit,
replacing it with self-doubt, hostility, hesitance, confusion and con-
flict, in fact, ironically, one of the greatest crimes one can commit

~

It is very difficult to respect or even for that matter
to take seriously those who have no clue or idea about
communication, or exhibit not an ounce of responsibility

~

Do not let your defeated thoughts get to you
because in fact in truth it is all those things
and stuff which led to that actual thought
and thus that thought (might just be false
or just a distorted form or the long-lost
result of the difference of loss) and not
be as bad as you may very well think

~

Those who constantly preach patience
are always the ones who make you
feel so nihilistic and impulsive and
end up doing some really crazy shit

~

Those who are pedantic present as overcompensating
from unresolved issues and conflicts and trauma from
their past; pompous, didactic with a clear clinical 'fear
of intimacy,' whereas ironically, paradoxically due
to these selfsame traits and characteristics, unable to
get close to people or things, thus a distorted thought
pattern so far from any resemblance or core set of facts

~

The babbling of a single phrase; those who speak
in absolutes, means absolutely nothing to me...

~

It's all those little things which push you over the edge
which are really not little but triggers from the head

~

More times than not, "the mind" plays the role of a thief
not petty, but complex and deep to help to contain the grief;
that pain and suffering to keep one's sanity and self-preservation
then all of a sudden out of nowhere (ironically like another type
of similar thief) a psychological and spiritual trigger happens
looking to steal everything in that one brief moment, usually
due to another either internal (fleeting feeling or emotion)
or external (image or language) resemblance of one of those
similar selfsame senses, and all the defenses (those coping
and survival mechanisms) that the thief (or mind) has naturally
developed, suddenly becomes uncovered, adopting something
of the mentality of a 'group home child,' exposed, fragile,
hyper-sensitive, and histrionic, almost going 'wild' wondering
why with a sense of nihilistic trepidation and existential high-
expressed emotion, so neglected, left deserted and abandoned

~

My 'guidance' counselor and dean of 'discipline'
used to say such things and make such sweeping

generalizations like I was 'acting-out' or 'attention-
seeking' but psychodynamically, how would I have
even known that if in fact that is what I was really
doing, and looking back retrospectively, what kind
of guidance or discipline was that really, and most
likely the exact reason why I was acting-out and
what do you call that? Attention-seeking?

~

People really go out of their way to not to get to know
each other and pass instant judgment based on their
own flimsy and fragile 'absurd' projecting; always
the exact people I don't want to get to know almost
like the bully in high school who still does not know
what to do with his anger, or the one, ironically, who
has been picked on way too long and strangely enough,
(almost parroting that behavior) eventually becomes just
as narrow-minded and impulsive in distorted thought pattern

~

Seduction and flirtation; what a strange and necessary way
to make a connection with the Homo-Sapiens I suppose better
than those suburban mothers filling up pinatas with rock candy
and taffy for their angelic monsters blindfolding them putting
bats in their hands and going swinging for the fences swingers
live in fences cut-throats killers and real estate agents as say
a sign of being successful out here is the closer your home
gets to the ocean but ironically become so much more distant
(defensive and indifferent as if you give a shit) people you
no longer have any interest and all their kids either become
princesses self-destructive or develop addictions mean-spirited
bitches walking with tennis racquets down private roads acting
like you give a fuck about them and want to fuck them nothing
could be further from the truth while they are the real rapists
(you find out with their strange sexual repression/fantasies
and husbands who stopped paying attention a long time ago)
looking to make their quota for the cathedral and country club

~

The court jester and king's fool
often know so much more and
so much more insightful cause
are forced to play by the rules

~

As a kid it was real easy being self-destructive (and klutzy)
Just try moving ahead (and making something...) after they
have taken everything which includes identity and meaning

The heart and soul were internal organs which felt out of order

~

Self-destructive behavior is that flashing trigger right
before you're about to reach the pinnacle of success

~

It is very easy to feel cursed when blessed
or vice-versa when surrounded by so many
vultures in a psychosocial environment of
an absurd and erratic impulsive behavior
or 'kill or be killed' aggressive human
nature often based on jealous and petty
insecurities, and will do 'practically'
anything humanly, often inhumanly
possible to control, abuse power,
cause conflict and take advantage

~

Ignorance causes people to rush to judgment
Arrogance, to run away from it...

~

O my god the things people judge you on
I can tell right away has absolutely nothing
to do with the process of judgment but rather
just really poor instincts and impulses (of their
own personal prejudice) and issues and conflicts
and losses which has absolutely nothing to do with it

~

The only thing the wild animal does not experience and feel
is sadness and guilt and remorse and conflict, which I kind
of think, cognitively, is not such a bad thing, as retrospectively
eventually, ironically, can't begin to tell you how much it has affected
and damaged me and taken my spirit and being; a sort of reverse evolution

~

In my opinion one of the worst things of all is family dysfunction
which gives a completely distorted view of reality (manipulations)
with absolutely no sense of fairness or justice, while all the little
people align together, more precisely in actual, clinical, didactic
terms where there is a literal reversal of roles between the child
and authority figure, often due to the latter's fragile identity, mal-
adaptive behavior (often some chemical dependency problem)
inability to communicate, or for that matter, function in 'the real
world,' and in the long-run, if enmeshed in it long enough, the
sincerely good and righteous soul becomes a victim or scape-
goat in this brutal and chaotic "kill or be killed" family system
(with a whole hell of a lot of humiliation with very little humility)
where they appear to care more about winning the battle than resolution

~

Neighbors are at best nuisances, nothing close to that ideal
of biblical (snoops you'd like to tie a noose) and more times
than not superimpose their issues onto you even start battles
over their own insecurities and shortcoming weaknesses

~

The ones with property will always be obsessively manicuring
it and never on it and those without will always come up with
the wrong conclusions and find ways to try and explore and
defile yours; an invasion of privacy is not only physical
but becomes psychological and spiritual as well

~

Out here don't know how to communicate at all
and got their guns and dogs and warning and no
trespassing signs, literally decked-out all around
their jungle gyms and Virgin Mary's and postage
stamp lawns, while strangely enough, these are the
ones who are accepted and fit in with good reputations

~

Marriage, get ready to be disinfected

~

The sound of utensils becomes maddening

~

You prefer to stay home to catch the sports and weather

~

No wonder in the end we turn to gardening and traveling!

~

The father at best (what happened to *Father Knows Best?*)
becomes a second, third class citizen with his wife and
kids dissing him, and must develop a double-life, while
turns to the comforts and solace of his office and basement

turns to making model planes and ships and cars
turns to stamp collecting and stocks and bonds

~

My drifting gondola
someone has already
picked up my luggage

~

I like bed & breakfasts sincerely but why
when you eat your breakfast in the morning
with the other guests they're always so formal
and polite and silent which I suppose is a good
thing and honestly got nothing against that when
you consider the other options yet just makes me
feel a bit melancholic and question my mortality even
feel slightly solemn where I just want to get out there
and ask the widow or the woman whose man walked out
on her can you please tell us where the dangerous parts are?

~

I spent my whole time with a girl on the ferry.
She told me she had spent the recent Summer
working at some wealthy French resort and
told me how snobby she thought the guests
were and was looking forward to returning
home and getting back as really missed
her family in Sicily. I had just gotten
off a rather maddening relationship
with a borderline girl who drove me
close to crazy and literally on-the-run
looking to forget her and in the back
of my mind was looking to spark up
another one on this ferry ride and
thought how cool would that be
(not to necessarily make love)
but just to spoon each other
in one of those lifeboats, two
strangers spooning each other
to eternity but I think she picked

up on this and sensed it and told
me she wasn't looking for anything
serious (nor was I) and I couldn't
help but to respect her and spent
the rest of the evening feeling so
lost and stranded deserted and
abandoned looking out to the
endless Mediterranean and
watching these Sicilians do
this horribly corny version
of slapstick Vaudevillian
with this very melodramatic Asian
crooner in a gold sequin jumpsuit
belting opera which made me feel
all that much more tragically lonesome

~

In the end it all seems
like some absurd post-
apocalyptic scene
from a Fellini movie
Chagall's angel crashing
into Mighty Mouse's
mistaken identity
just outside the
broken blinds of my
industrial stained
glass window in
delicious scents
of hot pretzels
& warm chest
nuts of Hell's Kitchen
still refuse aint to make
the runways any longer
at LaGuardia hell I'm still
willing to take that chance
on Expedia or Cheap-O Air
if it will get me back there anywhere
to Reno Nevada Palm Springs California
timber country just north of Seattle
in the torrential vagabond downpour
where they keep the old beat down
donut shops blow towering redwoods
getting buzzed off bear claws & cups

Joseph D. Reich

of joe; all those elements & moments
which make up melancholia; the me
and dew ring moonlight making loners
just like myself less lonesome; where's
my alchemist? Shaman? Bodhisattva
beautician all the way out in Brighton
Beach, Brooklyn who just makes all
miserable things of existence little
less burdensome massaging the
scalps of all those wise ass deli
wents & exhausted soiled Irish
brothers & laborers at day's end
with their arms collapsed contented
around each others shoulders scoping
them in strange awkward orgiastic pleasure
being vibrated liberated slightly grinning
leaned back in the barber chair without
a care, I swear in the glinting, glaring,
glimmering buttondown dusk window
on the avenue of Carrol Gardens when
the foghorns & church bells show up
out of nowhere in that one rare moment
of 'being there' high up there low down
there for those poor lost souls who
have been deserted & abandoned
done in from what life has done
to them a sort of sudden revelation
of instant-gratification & redemption
my only regret that ballerina who
used to hang her dripping braziers
like the tears of mythological sirens
on a clothesline beneath my apartment
for purposes of seduction & wanted me
to save her & be her savior from some
idiot boyfriend, but just didn't want to
play that role as felt a bit manipulative
& sleazy, getting back to my traveling
(can still taste baguette brie Kronenburg
Beer fresh piping take-out Vietnamese
no longer a colony no longer a
worried citizen finally at last
without a country literally
vanishing in thin air up
winding cobblestone
stairs of twilight
Monmartre where

they say they buried
a quarter of Jesus' heart)
back somewhere around
The Puget Sound between
America & Vancouver when
those silhouetted sacred sappy
logs go rolling freely like kindling
down midnight icy rivers beneath
ghostly bridges to unknown
miraculous destinations, O!
lo & behold! To be long-lost
& forgotten forever, a man
amen I mean a man can
dream can't he? Were you
being facetious? Literal?
Rhetorical? Attitudy?
& please don't tell me the
fog & mist & dew of dawn
doesn't have any aroma
the deep southern train
tracks of The Carolinas
& New Orleans from sweet
smelling sweltering stamen
of crepe myrtle & magnolia
those bleary-eyed puddles
of Lower East Side sidewalk
broken down boxcars refusing
to budge in tumbledown train
yards under the stars where
broke homeless senator's
sons study the bible & search
for jobs, diners & dogs con
veniently planted outside
the upsidedown shattered
skyline of Portland, Oregon
that stray salty sweet smelling
nomadic breeze sifting through
the hide & go seek thief streets
& cracked seams of solitary starving
lonesome San Francisco transient
lattice of Mission District where you
always runaway to & not a single soul
knows you except the bums & dope
addicts & hear the distant melodic
wail of seagulls faraway & familiar
on the holy whole Alcatraz Pacific

will always pick up your spirit
& open the heart & soul
& deliver you to sender
to tender stranger while no
need cuz already rescued
to take you to any place
specific or destination
as you're already there
broke & down ferry of
aristocrats & madmen
before it heads out to
long gone sea o say
can you see from
insane musty bustling
Athens Greece to those
whitewashed cliffs which
suddenly spring like some
breathtaking Atlantis offseason
from the Aegean sea from busy
Naples to the ragged rugged
glowing dawn of Sicily from
& dew la see 'ya to Afrique!
across the English Channel
to Lady Liberty sweeping
up the remains & holy
ashes of Chagall's angel
Mighty Mouse's leaking
diesel rubbing olive oil
into the aching belly of
some poor stray kitten
with once more that
swarm of half-crazed
hysterical seagulls who
always sense like stray
dogs & winos & manage
like madmen in the tragic
black & white static to stalk &
come bumrushing in from City
Island where you can always
get a good Sunday's fishing
in & The Mafia & Jews from
The Island always meet up
at sundown for great big
seafood platters which
include oysters rocky
fellow fried calamari

polenta endless carafes
of red wine laughter suntans
(where are those paramecium
I mean amoebas I mean single-
cell organism amphibians creeping
out of the ocean onto land for the very
first time to find life is just one gigantic
surf & turf platter on the most whitest
sand beach of all time in Ft. Walton
Florida to start off evolution where
a bleached blonde with a drinking
problem in some late-night bamboo
bar obviously drunk obviously alone rants
teary-eyed about her very intimate relationship
with God I mean where are those pristine petrified
conch shells just resting on the bottom of the sea
when mythological muscular Rastafarians without
an ounce of fat on them go diving in after them
in their cut-off jeans with machetes and clean
them out and make a fine fresh conch stew
with just a bit of hot sauce and lemon juice
all to be dipped into with a couple boxes of
Saltines at driftwood picnic tables beneath
ancient palm trees for the ritzy Club Med
like tourists just off the coast of Antigua
Antibes Entebbe The Taking
of Pelham 1,2,3...) all those
Jews from The Diamond District
& Sicilians from the fish market
piling back in with potbellies
& punchlines, eyes eternally
planted over shoulder keeping
an eye out for paybacks in long
lengthy, black & gold Cadillacs
like Batmobiles barreling home
to the land-o-lake, land of lost
lush & look-a-like suburbs
where dead ends look across
the whole blessed silent universe

~

I know this is the politically incorrect thing to say
but don't really care because always been about
as diverse and liberal as they come, as there are

certain groups these days that expect you to be
instantly sympathetic and supportive of them based
merely on their anacronym but are not necessarily
always so open-minded and welcoming (of your
individualism, how you've paid your dues, what
you've been through without a support system
or a particular group, been hurt, damaged,
personally disenfranchised, and alienated)
and often are quick to pass judgment and
jump to instant conclusions (also a certain
type of prejudicial and impulsive, exclusive
victimization) based on certain projections,
insecurities, traits and characteristics, while
ironically, paradoxically, not always so
compassionate and tolerant of your reality
as the real test of truth and integrity must
be based purely on sincerity and strength
of character, or vice-versa, and perhaps
even where "they" are and what they are
willing to do and contribute during periods of
crisis when you are feeling down in the dumps and blue

~

What kind of bullshit and nonsense is that political-correctness
telling us the proper (and formal) way of how to talk (and express
ourselves, and feel and act) and was made up by the biggest out-of-touch
jackasses in the first place, while was always so down-to-earth and quote on
quote diverse and never even thought about that nor the people I hung out with

~

The subtle shit that people say ain't subtle at all
and about as aggressive as they come
and what you learn upon reflection
and patterns turns to wisdom

~

Think about it! What a brilliant expression
a 'Freudian slip of the tongue' which pretty
much sums up the derivation of language,
all the subconscious, and civilization

~

When we say such declarative things like 'without a doubt'
we open ourselves up to doubt for the exact selfsame
reason and need we had to declare without a doubt

~

It is apparent we have no rights when we
instantly have to declare 'I have the right!'

Or how we interestingly derive opposite meaning (between
action and stagnancy) from such phrases like "takes place"

'Rain is expected.' What a weird type of thing to say
like that old cliché–"Patience is a virtue"

~

The words to the definition provide only a mildly fair description
to the essence and sentiment of the thing we are missing and don't
necessarily feel more complete, just a little less broken and empty

~

In reality 'inclement weather' doesn't really sound half-bad

~

I am going to invent a language
based on something that's never
been said before and when they
bring in the translator he's going
to say something that's never been
said before based merely on mood
and expressions and body language
like walking out that motel with her
the following morning in awkward
silence or staying in a relationship
for all the wrong reasons deconstructing
such things like nuance and mania and
racing thoughts and personification and

trying to put it all back together again
kind of like the weather but much
higher and much lower than one
of those award-winning weather
teams you see smiling all corny
and happily ever after on one
of those absurd billboards
before entering the Metropolis
team I've never trusted hoping
and praying before I die finding
something I do trust like this non-
language based on intuition perception
a sixth sense and something they can
never steal from me, nor even begin
to know finding that long-lost domicile
with my homegrown shot of morphine
moonshine and girl walking out that
motel door in awkward silence when
time stands still beneath that ribbon
of misty fog below the mountain

~

A rain on a pristine lake pours
within the windows of a cabin

Reflective, self-soothing

No need to go anywhere
at last contented…

~

There is a fine line yet huge schism between the resemblance
of the principle and notion of coincidence and superstition
like the selfsame confusion between the apparent images
and traits and characteristics of fate and mortality

~

People become atheists at very young ages

~

Reflection, revelations, and redemption...
Is there nothing better during periods of life-transition
when we feel helpless, have no control, and no ending?

~

I have even contemplated and had visions
of Summer during the harshest
conditions of Winter

~

Have planned great escapes and vacations with the imagination!

~

The immaculate and obsessively stripped-down exhibitionist humble
flamboyant cowboy in his chaps and sparkles and sequins and leather
boots and ten-gallon after a long weary night doing his rounds in Reno
pushes a supermarket cart and picks up the basic essentials for his foster
children and partner where an old miserable woman holding up the line
with her zombie-like power-struggles and treating the young, innocent
cashier like crap suddenly causes him out of nowhere to let out a wild
and liberating hooting-holler of "Whooop-di-do!" getting her out the
door and he takes off in his sparkles and sequins and leather boots
and ten-gallon happily ever after to that fine plush motel in the stars

He makes an honest living and not a
big believer in it's all about perception

~

An honest living like help wanted
looking for a high-end drug dealer
to distribute drugs to upper middle
class clients in The Upper West
and Upper East Side of Manhattan
clean record or criminal background
check not required nor necessarily to
be a team member or a "people person"

Joseph D. Reich

but a real individual with life experience
well-spoken with good bedside manner
good instincts and judgment (who does
not pass judgment) thrives under pressure
and in crisis situations and has the ability
to be sympathetic and develop trust
amongst clients…get full access
to company bicycle and the pool
at 92nd St Y, make your own hours!

~

I could never stand those people who would make
such grandiose proclamations like 'get your priorities
straight' like how dare you and who the hell was even asking
and how would you even know what they were in the first place?

~

What kind of crap is that
just think of that phrase
and proclamation and re-
peat it over and over again

Make a name for yourself
Make a name for yourself
Make a name for yourself
Make a name for yourself

as it almost seems to instantly
betray and contradict every
logical law of linguistics
language and semantics

Why looking back at my childhood
I saw myself as a passionate thief
with mad heart and soul and never
trusted those with good judgment

~

Don't play with semantics
What are the other options?

~

How statistics and demographics do more to remove you
from the actual intimate object and provide less clarification
than their obvious and biased conclusions for the selfsame
reason of their abstract reasoning and absolute conviction
to why any of this was even studied or researched in the first
place in the attempts to draw a conclusion and make a point

Contrary, idealistically, every real and true 'thriving democracy'
is based on a fine and open-minded aesthetic, embedded into
the natural framework and solid foundation of a system of fairness;
self-aware, sensitive, objective and receptive (giving the impression
of free will and volition, however realistic between policy and practice)
like the presentation of pleasant (even provocative) architecture in the topo-
graphy and lay of the land, while its inhabitants, through this selfsame image and plan,
having the ability to thrive and function, become a reflection of this breadth and vision

~

'The institution' of democracy does not really work
when in fact it is too democratic as it stands as
(for) a pure microcosm and reflection of human
nature, which in truth and in reality, is rather
impulsive and aggressive and animalistic, and
eventually, based on these selfsame, brutish
'kill or be killed' traits and characteristics, if there
is no real checks and balances system (on a punitive,
humanistic, and systematic level) to regulate it, the
grand con-artist, the megalomaniac and madman will
somehow find a way to take advantage, so in fact what
we do have now is some real-life satire and nightmare
come true in America and the madmen (the blind men)
have not only taken over the asylum, but the blinds
have been pulled down in the steeple, as well as the
radio stations, TV commercials (collective unconscious)
universities and government which has only been building
up because no one has really been strong enough or for
that matter, courageous (call them what you want, a rebel
or patriot) to do anything about it, and important, as well, to
stay away from such instant panaceas, verbiage, or labels as
'movements' because does more to commercialize and dilute it

~

Indifference is a slow-death and the worst sort of neglect

~

If only man were a little less attention-seeking
and paid a little more attention to his character

~

We make jokes and riddles in attempts to cope with our mortality
(often in denial or deflecting from other's neglect and complacency)

~

Keeping the faith is far harder than any such statement

~

I'll take instinct, intuition, and a sixth sense any day
over what they claim to be of substance and meaning

~

There is a futile absurdity in questioning morality
because those who we so desperately need to attach it
to (for reasons maddening and come up with solutions)
would never even think of it, never ever be a part of their
being or cross their consciousness; that is the perverse
paradox when we speak of the concept of morality

~

Too many are rotten or as Chuck D. stated–
'I know some of them are just goddamn devils'
while you're just trying to mind your own business
(and find some peace & quiet, solitude and contentment
in this existence) and they'll still try to rape and violate
you any chance they can, and when you just naturally react

the dishonest cowards that they are, will try and play possum
and act like you were the provocateur, aggressive and crazy one

~

While ultimately, inextricably, in the long-run
in the end, the very end, how alone and lonely
and lonesome the real true-blue hero must get
for all he is forced to tolerate, put up with and
to accept, as they will all exhibit the exact
same characterological and behavioral
symptoms and patterns, and traits and
characteristics of jealous (they will always
do things from a distance) while all they
can present and all they can be is trivial
and petty and (act-out, hostile and passive-
aggressive) for their own shortcoming
weaknesses, insecurities, lack
of self-worth, and self-respect

~

He always plays the role of savior or martyr...
You wash yourself below the factory waterfall

~

The child of a clinical narcissist ends up becoming
the result and manifestation of that brilliant, keen
Johnny Rotten line "ever feel like you been cheated?"
as without even being aware or knowing it (meeting
the criteria for all psychological and spiritual victims)
and the characterological and behavioral pattern of
acting-out and fulfilling the 'self-fulfilling prophecy'
often self-destructive, more times than not, suicidal
with no real sense of self; of self-worth or self-respect
or core identity, while taking it even one step further
than the conclusions of the sociologists or psychologists
will unconsciously, as a child or adolescent, always find
themselves in active-conflict with those similar, symbolic
authority figures who subjugated or took advantage of them
(and questioning and testing) and 'can't stay out of trouble'
and rebelling (stealing and taking back from every entity

and authority figure) for all that has been taken and stolen
from them (unconsciously, subconsciously, parroting those
behaviors) while also too this is how they feel empowered
(feel alive and exist and thrive) function and move forward

~

You really start to feel lonesome when those
who were supposed to protect you (or play
those roles) are 'clueless,' insensitive,
and self-absorbed, and then experience
the phenomenon of feeling lost forever

~

Why don't they have anniversaries
for like when people commit suicide
and put that amount of candles on
the cake for how hard they tried
for how far they were able to make
it and each year keep on moving
backwards to the age when they
conceive they may have been happy?

~

I have a specific theory and hypotheses and not to at all
sound glib or insensitive, but think certain people try
to commit suicide often based on their baseline and
just like that 'super-saturation point' where you add just
one more particle to the formula everything just falls out;
of course it obviously can do with a chemical imbalance
or something physiological and severe and situational
(and impossible and overbearing circumstances) but
why do we so often hear when probing friends and
acquaintances and family members they can't believe
he/she did it, because seemed to be so contented (in
such a good and happy place) but my hypotheses is for
this exact selfsame, perverse reason where they suddenly
at that moment or juncture developed the confidence and
energy and motivation, almost 'coming to terms with it'
more dexterous with less resistance (having to do with

that baseline and super-saturation point) that it's just not
ever going to get any better than this, and 'not worth' it

~

The subconscious is brutally honest
while often turns to an unconscious
conscious liar and con-artist on his
knees throwing bones somewhere
between his fate and mortality

~

Over-politeness often takes on the form
of self-flattery, playing possum, self-
interest and reactive-formation, which
is a defense-mechanism, that implies
where someone can put their arm around
you and exclaim–'I love this guy!' really
deep-down inside, loathing and despising

~

Politics really has absolutely nothing to do with politics
but so much more the philosophy and psychodynamics
and hypocrisies and contradictions of erratic human nature and
what man is willing to do to gain an advantage without contrition

~

Politics is simply an extension
a reflection and microcosm
of poor character

~

To say it is a convenient form of amnesia
or 'might over right' might be one of the biggest
understatements of all time like that of the alcoholic
when they are under the influence with their Dr. Jekyl
& Mr. Hyde erratic behavior and if you should happen to

remind them of this or somehow bring it to their attention
go on the instant defensive and clinical denial, on the all
out attack and get hostile, thus must align and thrive and
function by a very absurd and fragile herd-like mentality

~

The real true-blue martyr and rebel rebels
(maintains and keeps on) against all stigmas
and stereotypes of how he was mislabeled or falsely judged

~

Has anyone ever been pebbled to death? I have!
(which to me implies being stuck in an unfair
and unjust, bureaucratic system where you'll
eventually always be underestimated and
misinterpreted by those who ironically
don't even know how to interpret the law
and will in the long-run more times than
not overcompensate and abuse power,
brutish and futile, based on peripheral
prejudicial reasons) So yes! I've been
pebbled to death, pestered and peppered
and pelted by the petty people of existence
like when they arrest you for mistaken identity
and stop your yellow taxi driving graveyard shift
(trying to make an "honest" living) and simply
ask him why he's stopping me and nail you for
resisting arrest and eventually come out of the
paddywagon and tell you to remove your shoe
laces (like I even give a damn and would try
anything) and when they let you out the next
morning and of course never apologize while
the sarcastic and sadistic c.o.'s (brave men in
blue) spent the whole previous night mocking
and ridiculing and trying to put the fear of God
into you, and can't really explain the following
morning after they release me a mistaken identity
(after police harassment) and get fired I swear from
two jobs and so yes people do get stoned to death
but also not so uncommon to be pebbled as well

~

I find often I have the coping or survival skills
(or for that matter even street smarts) to get
through certain phases and episodes of trauma
but it's the shit later on that presents itself during
periods of peaceful, subtle, stagnant days whether
in everyday functioning or just suddenly showing
up out of nowhere in my nightmares and dreams

~

I am keenly interested on a clinical and empirical level
when psychological triggers actually begin to take form
after periods and phases of severe crisis, struggle, and
profound trauma and suppose has a little something to do
with one's own psychological composition and disposition
(whether fragile or acquired) and survival skills and coping
mechanisms after somehow 'getting through it' in a period
of cognitive stasis, solitary reflection, contemplation, isolation
and even asceticism, perhaps having some genuine, consistent
downtime after the natural and instinctive defenses are down and
when it all finally 'kicks in' during brooding, subconscious avoidance,
engaging in daily activities, or one's abstract and concrete state of being

i.e. One wonders as well from a physiological or phenomenological point
of view how one would make the distinction or draw similarities between
the sudden appearance of the psychological trigger and the subconscious?

~

Often triggers become triggers to triggers to triggers
not necessarily always out of (stemming from)
something profound or traumatic, but from a
repetitive kind of dwindling down, decay of
'the soul,' existential emptiness and neglect

~

The institution of religion, historically, psychologically
and spiritually, one of the greatest of double-standards

~

One's mortality is challenged and put in question
when surrounded by constant vultures who
wouldn't think twice about taking it…

A matter of fact more times than not, thrive off it

~

One thing I'm sure about is dread and doubt

~

The possible (act of) freedom (or free will and volition)
is having the ability to perceive and picture it
and thus, then, one day to attain it

~

We all perish during the presentation of the smallprint
or those commercials over the radio where they read
a mile a minute (punitively are covered)
and the audience can't keep up with it

~

What happens when we live in a generation where 'Big Brother'
has become a 'live' human being, but not really, because these
days, the way they have been meticulously and pathetically
commanded and trained no longer contains any real human
qualities (or element) or attributes of judgment, intuition or
instincts, and thus absurdly, ironically, even tragically, does
not meet the criteria or competency of that great big grand
computer in the sky (as if the heart and soul's been converted
backwards and it n/a no longer applies) and they have all been
pleasantly placated and brainwashed (by some brand new amor-
phous conglomerate out in Utah) as well as to read and fill in
the spaces directly off the telemarketer script of validating
the human being's feelings and emotions, and say such shit
mechanical, pre-manufactured, like–"Sir, I can see how that
can be…" or "I can really relate" finding yourself getting more

frustrated and irate, insulted and offended (by some obnoxious
obvious, see-through, cookie-cutter representative and can't help
but to be mildly reactive and sarcastic) when you just wanted
EST Eastern Standard Time, from their false advertising for
them to actually convert the measurements from the size of
the image you see conveniently distorted on the screen from
cubic centimeters (something crazy and non-reality-based like
60,000) to simple inches and feet for a bookshelf to go on your son's
wall, while you hang up the phone (on the automaton) cursing involved

~

Often 'the bad boy' is not as bad as he may very well seem
and when you really get to know him, one of the nicest and
kindest and most compassionate and giving of human beings
far more "human" than any one of these driven good-deed doing
volunteering individuals for their resumes or non-profit agencies
rather aggressive and alienating in how they're always 'desperately'
proving and self-promoting and how they want others to perceive
them to be; in all of these absurd cases, it really does come
down to politics and promotion and good and bad publicity

~

Self-righteous virtue (passive-aggressive
and hostile) is a certain form of evil

~

Often when I'm struggling or perseverating with a specific crisis or conflict
it is always the surreal or a metaphor which gets me through it, and then
will assign (or think up) another metaphor for that metaphor and attempt
to objectively analyze and access their similar traits and characteristics
and then its differences, and instantly go back to the original problem
and dilemma or cognitive semantics and definition which was causing
such a spiritual schism, and find almost through the processes and
dynamics of 'desensitization' and 'partialization' heals and provides
a panacea to the manic core of that specific high-expressed emotion

~

I think deep down on the most shallow of levels
often how I feel is exactly how I don't feel and
always been one of the most intense passionate
purists of intuitive opposites or cautious and guarded
of those who speak in absolutes which always felt like
something of a perverse manipulation or brainwash
of the soul of a certain sort of ethics and morals to
simplistically be a part of or slave to the status-quo

~

Sometimes I believe the tangible action and sensation
and phenomenon and concept of love to be so much
more than all that has been imagined and thought.
Sometimes I believe its symbolic and perceived
loss and then sudden heroic archetypal 'saving
and redemption' to be more than its actual
natural core. Sometimes I believe what we
conceptualize and conceive to be the image
(or even sudden spontaneous flash) of its beauty
to be so much more that the elements of its folklore.
Sometimes I believe in the short-term and long-run
love to simply be the savior of all that we have lost

~

I believe the sadness of living or mortality
lies in the fragility of the missing pieces
of the puzzle (which got broken somewhere
along the line...) somewhere between here
and the constellations; is that fate? (futility)?
Who said that? Shakespeare? Moliere?
Tennessee Williams? Eugene O'Neill?

~

Has that very spiritual rhetorical question
ever been answered, can I get a witness?
Have they ever found out that individual
who didn't let in the inn Mary Magdelan?
Civilization simply implies you gotta pay

taxes; there's a constant might over right
mentality, and that gossip and rumors will
always supersede the truth like superstition
and religion over the independent thinker

~

I always could never stand those types of people or acquaintances
or colleagues, who acted like martyrs with savior complexes, who
when you were going through a life-transition (even honestly which
happened to be good and benign) would say such things like–"I was
praying for you" as my first instinct always was mind your own business
I don't need any type of praying, sincerely, or whoever said I asked you
to pray for me, and pray for yourself and your own issues, or however
that works (ironically, always turned out to be the clinical narcissists
or fellow colleagues in the therapy field who were the ones, interestingly
who always talked way too fast or loud and wouldn't let you get a word
in edgewise) and what kind of bizarre, random proclamation is that to
make anyway, while paradoxically, ironically always ended up instead
feeling violated, as is not this ritual and dynamic, too, supposed to be
intimate and confidential, and again who the heck even asked you to
pray for me in the first place (like some sort of distorted blind date or that
old cliche "stop flattering yourself") like some strange, perverse passive-
aggressive form of control and reactive-formation (the African-Americans
always came up with the most poignant and profound expressions like
'act like you know' or 'don't play yourself') and by the way, how do
you know I believe in God, man, or for that matter, even yourself?

~

That whole concept and phraseology from those children's stories
and fables and parables of living 'happily ever after' was all really
based on some sort of wish/fantasy sublimation (form of escapism)
as the characters and themes and plotlines, and what they had to
withstand and endure from a nihilistic, ascetic, and symbolic point
of view, was all so violent and miserable, and even if one was to
repeat that phrase of happily ever after over and over again from
a musical, structural, and phonetic point of view, sounds so
foreign and unfamiliar (and all so distant and unrealistic
and untrue) all written to teach the child and adolescent
a very Dickensian and Draconian moralistic and ethical
lesson to be imbued into their subconscious, but often
so savage and sadistic (causing the story to take on a
whole different strange life and mythology of its own)
as the child, most likely, gets confused and conflicted

between the imagination and real-life fear and trepidation
with this perverse, overwhelming 'might over right' theme
and concept (without perhaps the raconteur even knowing
it and even too much for the adolescent's coping and survival
mechanisms to deal with) not exactly sure what is learned
and how it is processed (while more times than not, parroted
and acted-out) and wonder if perhaps, if somewhere down the line
its benign intentions as well as phraseology of unrealistic expectations
of 'happily ever after' does not do more harm and damage than good?

~

There is a certain tragic melancholia in love
as our intuition and senses; our imagination
(and ability to dream) becomes so much more
pronounced and keen in keeping with the natural
rhythms of nature, always causing a schism and
conflict being forced back into a culture which is
so mundane and monotonous, and operates and
functions with predictable patterns of routine and
ritual where deep down inside could 'take it or leave it'

~

Romance is everything removed and forgotten
right at that exact moment and an explosion of
love and the senses that cannot be penetrated

~

Serving tea on her pretty knees...
Everything else took her self e'steam

~

We fall madly in love with things we just miss and almost got
or got too much of it and took off like a thief in the night...

~

We live our lives somewhere
between the flicker of a flame
and the tick-tock of a clock
there's a fine line between
being a criminal and saint
and knowing who's full
of shit and who's not
devils are those
who steal spirit
angels, well, some
sort of soul survivor

~

It's a weird thing this thing called survival...
a matter of fact makes absolutely no sense at all
the people are not palpable and mostly just play roles
and things far more tangible such as the change of seasons
the remains of the peaceful lingering puddles which fell
from the sky that always allows for reflection and to realize
the strafing of the low iridescent clouds over the mountain
the shivering dancing shadows outside your window with
the hissing of wind and crow flying low across the world
wondering exactly when he came into being and can relate
so much more to the freak and madman giving it their all
just trying to make their way across town than any one
of those know-it-all clowns who try and make you feel
small like you don't belong and a bunch of punks and pussies
who have no experience at all and show up with their issues
over your local cable that slaughterhouse by the raging river
flowing under the bridge where the delinquents and angels
live and blow big purple bubbles when the boxcars come in

~

How to get that spirit
back fly off the high
way into town in
to the mountains

~

Down in that part of downtown
you can drive through certain
parts of downtown and drive
through drive-thru's and pick
up a pint of bourbon, can drive
through and pick up a safe and
secure box of bullets, can drive
through and be instantly absolved
and forgiven; a couple Hail Mary's
here, couple Rosary's there and you're
a 'new man'; well that's a democracy
if I've ever heard of one…Isn't it?

~

I feel like the remnants of a vaudeville punchline
after having gotten the infamous hook and
best friends turn on you pale frail naked
flaming red head through the keyhole
of that motel you were willing to throw
it all away for in a life of one-night stands
a doggy bag from The Coliseum uninvited
to Jesus' Last Supper the leftovers at one
of those dinner theaters hey did you hear?
Who's got the fondue? Who's got the
pu pu platter? Who's got the message
and messenger and poster for Jesus'
crucifixion? Boys staking their territory
by spitting same insane three-headed
monster on the corner who never
left the neighborhood throwing quick
and clever pick-up lines at rush hour
trying to pick up all the prime women
who can't help but feel flattered ("send
me to the corner I've been very bad!")
Baseball bat and blindfold and pinata
also good in later life (taking practice
swings blindly) for those phases when
they out of nowhere just up and leave
you the tickertape caption below the
Puerto Rican weatherwoman to die
for just simply reads–"Rowdy"

~

Standing in profile
3:02 in the morning
my mugshot in front
of the bright light of
refrigerator catching
the college scores
from the night
before like the
FBI's 10 most
wanted stuck up
against the post
office wall
wanted dead
or alive but
feel neither
wanted nor
dead or alive

~

In dreams it seems like we're always asking permission
where we're not only the audience, but also the 'soul'
protagonist; is not this paradoxical and perverse
dynamic us looking into our subconscious?

~

I remember this Bukowski poem
don't quite remember it exactly
where he was doing this poetry
reading on some college campus
and when he was done stumbling
drunk all alone across the quad
in the middle of the evening
just trying to make it home
and looking back at that poem
somehow find this image for my
insomnia cathartic and liberating

Joseph D. Reich

~

Been so broke recently thinking
of using our tax return money
for a trip to Vegas would that
be considered tax evasion
onomatopoeia po-lice! or
whatever the hell you call it
Any which way been going on
Expedia practically every single
day not necessarily directly on
the strip with those loud drunken
screaming idiots in the hall but
a little off with a nice refreshing
pool for the wife and kid and a
panoramic view of the mountains
in what's that desert called The Mojave
when the sun goes down and pastel
lights just naturally come into being

~

That convenient expression of "history has a tendency
to repeat itself" is about as accurate as the selfsame traits
and characteristics of those (self-absorbed idiots) who ironically
bring about its derivation and fruition (and even futile repetition)

~

Almost every war did not start from that source
or proverbial boundaries crossed but all those so
called principles and morals which came before

~

I used to work at a place called Soho Books
on West Broadway in Soho, New York
and my boss was a real nice guy from
The Island half-Irish half-Italian who
was married to a good looking Indian
woman and we used to go all out for him
cause he treated us like humans and saw
all the seasons pass in front of that door

the first Winter snows the leaves blowing
in from Autumn the madman from Summer
and fake decadent rich kids from nightclubs.
One time during one of those workdays we
got our stock in we got a book about how to
build a dinosaur out of chicken bones and used
to be something of a running and ongoing joke
yet looking back in retrospect do believe very
profoundly and poignantly having to do with
the nature of mortality its natural collapse
and the diligent and determined attempts
to try and build it all back (brittle and delicate) from
a physiological psychological sentimental perspective

~

What a waste of time in certain people I've wasted my time
but in looking back just as guilty in my selfsame desire to try
and discover and find (save and redeem similar exact things)
through probing and inquiring by intrinsic nature and design

~

For all those character recommendations never quite exactly sure
if they had good character or that boss or supervisor if he/she had
good character and good judgment to judge the character recommendations
and thus in the long-run to judge mine, and usually somewhere down the line
a little ways into the interview with far more real-life experience and streetwise
and them finding the need and compulsion to make certain alignments (I think
wanting me to be included and a part of, of which I had absolutely no desire)
crossing boundaries and breaking confidences (not by coincidence in the near
to remote future exhibiting these exact same patterns) not exactly sure what
I was getting myself into, but deep-down inside probably knew exactly and
how in the long-run and denouement, I would be the fall guy; how the ones
on top always manage to keep their jobs while the CEO's (the board
of 'trustees') know how desperate they are in how much they
need them, running things for them, for these false gods

~

Almost every job I have ever interviewed for convinced
me how much of a con it all was and that specific manager

or supervisor just came off as some sleazy sort of used car
salesman pretending to make an offer never heard before

~

When they made the offer it always felt so gross and vulgar
like when you were young and some girl suddenly declared
she had a crush on you, or becoming a part of some
dysfunctional family you know you want no part of

~

Almost every job I ever began always felt like
an instant 'us against them' environment of
dysfunction, guarded and defensive about
how you would fit in or how you might
threaten (or even that matter how you
might 'save' them) and could always tell
right there in the moment, didn't have too
much to do with merit (or fairness) or even
for that matter a heck of a lot of professionalism

~

Family dysfunction becomes like a cut-throat competition
where no one wins and everyone loses (where they some
how care more about engaging in the power-struggle and
winning the battle not giving a damn about losing the war)

~

Can one seek redemption or full enlightenment
if they cannot ever forgive themselves
(being very tough on themselves)?

That there is always the eternal, existential conflict
but what if you spent a full, thorough, solitary life
going it alone, trying to attain knowledge?

Is that not enough?

~

Father pleasantly regresses. Goes to his kid's dorm room
when he isn't there. Looks into his mini-fridge. And grabs
a couple dutch-apple Pop Tarts. Cans of Coors beer. Throws
on a Grateful Dead record. Could be American Beauty or
Workingman's Dead. And coils in the fetal position. And
hopes to heal all pain and damage and alienation which
originally was done there. Reads those deep sociological
and philosophical books off his silly bus. Used to read books
off other kid's silly bus he found interesting and not off his.
And would never go to class. Put on probation so far from
anything having to do with fraternities and The Deep-South.
Spending his dusks and early evenings racing streetcars on
his bicycle (desperately hoping to enter other dimensions)
exploring those sidestreets and burntout dangerous areas
of real-life leftover spirits and phantoms. Even those under
ground antique shops and second-hand stores of long-lost
labyrinth subterranean tunnels of New Orleans. Returning
back from below sea-level starving and somehow far more
spiritual than anything having to do with a higher-education
and one of those perfect privileged well-rounded individuals.
Father leaves a note on the mini-fridge and thanks him for
the shelter and sanctuary. And disappears lost and found
back down the highway a new man far different and exactly
the way he was way before he ever went to places like this

~

In the very end hopefully we can look forward to looking backwards
to periods (and phases) and times when things were free and true
and were not controlled too much by superstition and ritual

~

All those infamous great scholars and philosophers
love to rant and rave how it's all really about perception...
I've had enough perception to last a lifetime and what's really
perception anyway when you really stop to think about it? If you
ever stop to think about it? Think about it! (as when you consider
its opposite, really not so much different than the ignorant, impulsive
people processing or not processing) Did Peter Pan ever find his shadow?
Probably planted somewhere in Plato's cave between yesterday and tomorrow

~

I think Heaven or Hell will be like that *Odd Couple*
episode where Oscar and Felix go on that game show
and are forced to choose behind some closed door and
just like everything else get a lifetime supply of canned squid

~

Baking peanut butter chunk cookies
hearing myself humming–"All I need
in this life of sin is me and my girlfriend"

~

After an
insane day
I decide out
of nowhere
to just start singing
in my easy chair
to her good ole
Billy Idol and
was able to reach
all the high-pitched
howls then ended
with some of his
love ballads
thought baby
after we just
lose it all
why not
just pick
up a couple
wild roosters
hens, sheep
and goat
a pair
of live
llamas
although
we got no
idea how
to raise

& take care
of them but
neither did
they for us
idea I had of
having that
good ole
reel to reel
projector
& projecting
beaming light
onto the side
of our barn
for the townsmen
The Marx Brothers
The Bowery Boys
Blue Hawaii
The King &
I & then just
once a Summer's
night Shakespeare's
tragedies beneath
the stars with that
fine cheap wine
you can only
pick up at
Walmart & if
don't do it right
can bean us
with rotten
vegetables
like they
did to
The Little
Rascals
and when
it all comes
down to it it's
all about that
video by Billy
Idol your eyes
without a face
which to me
always had
that keen
mysterious

romantic moon
like quality which
always remained
indelibly etched
in your memory

~

Per
son
icky
ayyy!
self
mute
i late
when
can't
self
mode
evade
like
that
poor
black
girl
belting
gospel
in the
middle
of Grand
Central
Station
for her
crack
habit
has a
habit
has a
habit
has a
habit
in this
habitat
to fell
low

some
mad
made
routine
& ritual
can't get
out of
in this
existence
existdance
just trying
to go the
distance
taking
the local
back
with all the
murdering
madmen
through
the cracked
window of
the ghetto
got to go!
got to go!
god to go
back to
their
illusions
which are
delusions
of grandeur
& persecution
to keep them
grounded
with the sun
going down
over the
platform
over the
town
over the
foghorns
over the
longing
& count

Joseph D. Reich

down of
daze of
dreams
of in
sane
mort
ality

~

In the end
we simply
coil in the
fetal position
like the steam
swirling from
faraway familiar
smokestacks
on the river
in the warmth
of winter in
The Lower
East Side,
Queens,
Brooklyn,
those towns
on the horizon
always blinking
in bleak beautiful
postmodern
desolation
Detroit,
Philadelphia,
New Orleans
falling in love
with that traveling
nurse practitioner
a tall thin angel
taking your vitals
looking like she's
never been touched
before murmuring
Buddhist prayers
medium-rare
existence of

a postman having
made something
of himself his
only regret
witch comes
back to haunt
him his son turning
into a dope addict
while all that's left
is to read the funnies
and obituaries with
the day disappearing
over the silhouetted
factories, trainyard
and holy hospital
the last time
he will fold up
the newspaper
in The Bronx
having lost
his mind
might be
something
just like
a rebirth

~

In looking back at those phases of our existence
with a certain amount of sentimental fondness
it is not just the images, but also the dialect
and language, and cadence and musicality
of tones of voices and undying reliable
companionship like the unconditional
whimsical eternal seasons; sincerity
measured in earthen tones and
everything you did after school
right around dusk and sundown

~

Never underestimate the influence of the rain...
Yes the sun has built great societies and civilizations
but the rain allowed us to contemplate and realize them

Joseph D. Reich

~

The wrong people show up to the hoedown
It's the swingers I mean the ones who like
to dance swing I mean the ballroom dancers
They say that Fred Astaire
and Ginger Rogers in real
life didn't like each other
What is real life anyway
and how is that the case as
they were made for each other
They said that Marlon Brando
was a bad fighter and used
to love to play practical
jokes on his leading
ladies and drive them crazy
Jimmy Cagney and Humphrey
Bogart used to stay out
all night and literally
before their sets get
wrecked and into brawls
The first immigrants crawled
off the boat in black & white
and there were still Indians
and fur traders in downtown
Manhattan before the Dutch
came and made their dutch
cobblestone and named
it New Amsterdam
The Jews were the first Mafia
even before the Sicilians
even before the Chinese
took over Hester and they
took over Mott Street
The best Little Italy is
uptown in The Bronx
smaller and more
intimate and
economical
and no tourists
I gotta before
I bite the dust
get back to Andalucia
already made it to Sevilla
and just want to do Cordoba
don't care how I get there

even if I'm The Great One
Jackie Gleason playing
The Poor Soul or lending
his handkerchief to Naughton
grumbling–"it's for showing and
not blowing" Audrey Hepburn having
escaped those drug dealers and killers
in her NYC basement apartment a blind
woman ditching her throne on her Roman
Holiday and Cary Grant up in the Technicolor
Monte Carlo rooftops & stars having become
suave having grown up a poor kid and acrobat
in the circus in later life a desperate romantic
trying to find the right girl developing
an addiction tripping on acid Bella Lugosi
nodding-out Spencer Tracy with his drinking
problem and Steve McQueen appetizing on a
bunch of different leading Hollywood ladies in
reality something of a stud and heroic stuntman
always jealous for some reason of Paul Newman
believing he deserved as much props and attention
the opposite of Greta Garbo wanting to be forgotten
having a difficult time making the distinction between
W.C. Fields and Winston Churchill (hey just realized they
had the same initials) twirling his top hat on top of his
cane in front of the exuberant masses in post-victory
The Bowery Boys below and deathwish D.W. Griffith
up in the air teetering and tip-toeing without a care
on top of a topless girder putting up a smoggy
skyscraper in 1920's America as believe my
existence at best was Curly Stooge taking
some truth or dare from one of his Yiddish
cousins from Brooklyn who got all frustrated
and slapstick as a defense-mechanism
What happened to Adolphe Menjou
and Edward G. Robinson?
Donna Reed like a flower
and Jimmy Stewart playing
that psychotic rabbit Harvey?

~

History like home movies like the story of reality
This slow-motion film going in fast-forward…

That Leftover Gold Dust In The Parking Lot Of Early Dusk

all of those banktellers & pharmacists
i end up getting attached to always end up
moving back to boston or their hometown of ohio

i want a transfer
to 1973
key biscayne, fla.

The Hx Of Mankind & Civilization

anna freud
i'm a scared!
anna freud
i'm a scared!
anna freud
i'm a scared!
anna freud
i'm a scared!

Working Methadone

he used to wear his pimping sky-blue
shag fur coat to the methadone clinic

he was a real nice kind and good guy
just trying to survive like the rest of us

think he was puerto rican…

and used to get some of the cutest and most beautiful
angels you'd ever see in the projects to do his bidding

almost like some gigantic sign or advertisement
along the highway or when arriving at the airport

"try heroin"

he i guess just like myself had realized and discovered
through experience and wisdom it was all just about

the dose you took somewhere between self-determination
and self-preservation and yeah i guess all in moderation

i casually asked him what he was planning on doing
over the weekend and very quick and clever

almost in a juvenile manner just shot back–
"i'm gonna play the game of life!"

wasn't sure if he was being serious…

A Different Sort Of Autobiography

Part 1

--"i just wanted to hear a sweet pretty voice on the other end of the line"

--"yes sir, you've reached the luxor right on the strip in the heart of vegas"

--"can you send me a color brochure?"

Part 2

if patience is a virtue
i must be jesus–
"vegas baby! vegas..."

Part 3

i look up at god like a coin
being tossed in the air...

Part 4

people's closure often is like some sort of cruel indifference

(while even i got my ear tugged by the dean of discipline
putting all my peers in hysterics, mumbling in mock-tone
that song by that brilliant alternative rock band, the smiths–

"i've seen it happen in other people's lives
and now it's happened in mine..."

Part 5

i have fallen in love with my son's swim instructor
(who has a body and spirit to die for) and love how
she's completely indifferent and pays me no mind

the rest of the white people out here seem too self-
absorbed and try way too hard in their efforts towards
a klutzy (and passive-aggressive hostile) form of sarcasm

Part 6

who came up with that idea back in the day to take a gorilla
and put him in a cage and take samsonite luggage and have
him toss it all over the place to show how it could in no way
be battered or damaged and somehow thinking back to that
image feels like something rather comforting and cathartic

Part 7

when you get a little bit older
you find they become a little colder
a little less sincere or more see-through
and fair-weathered like one of those commercials
for "starving artists" at the hyatt convention center

located at the airport where they always give you very
specific directions and the exact hours on the weekend
with all those horrible pastel reprints of landscapes
or sunsets or waves crashing down on shore to be
put up in lonely chain motels to meet your quota

they all end up very single-minded and goal-oriented
while you ironically starving maybe like one of those
continental breakfasts of a roll a pad of butter and
small glass of orange juice looking just like those
pastel waves crashing down on shore at sundown.

Swallowing Your Pride Chasing It
With Something Even More Depressing

I.

He used to love how she'd just stand on that back porch
force her face up to the darkening tremulous clouds and arch
her back and whole body and being up into the blue downpour

and would keep on dancing more and more
joyously liberated howling mad out loud and
the more and more it came down the less she gave
a damn if she got struck by the lightning and thunder

a stripper who'd leave her poor shredded slippers
outside the screen door on the back porch...

Having too experienced a whole lifetime
and existence of spiritual and psychological
trauma he was able to completely relate to her
and love her even that much more in times like these

and even though he knew it could only last so long
and at best be ephemeral how these emotions
and fleeting moments would last forever

II.

He thought back to all those friends
who had borrowed books and tapes
from him and knew probably somehow
somewhere in the back of his mind
would never ever see them again

but had he not too borrowed a couple
himself and thought was not maybe
this like the grand metaphor for life
making all these transient sentimental
and heartfelt exchanges no less the wiser
eventually becoming a man of slight wisdom

III.

He had taken in all of La Rochefoucald's "Maxims"
and The Mamas & The Poppas and Joni Mitchell

IV.

And strangely in the end probably having something
to do with that damage and concept of mortality
(and romance and fantasy) ironically thought
back most profoundly to those fleeting
and histrionic relationships like with
that stripper than the ones which
were supposed to represent
stability and all things
substantial which felt
ironically so much
more superficial.

Bewitching Hour Or Time Of Prayer

Wild coyote shows up to our screen door
with a record player strapped to his back
and a scratchy record full of static that
spins round and round and repeats over
and over–"Come out with your hands up!
Come out with your hands up!" and leave
him some leftover boneless spareribs and
he gobbles it up and see him take off back
to the darkening forest of folklore; put pork rinds
on the sill for visitors; most especially carrier pigeons
until in the long-run the ignorant, suspicious status
quo who have tried to outsmart us finally leave us
alone realizing we're just minding our own business
trying to make it and that's all we've ever done simply
trying to make names for ourselves; the telemarketers
reading straight off their scripts at dusk during the supper
hour ring the phone having set up a trigger of straight-up
heavy breathing hardcore porn or some mechanical man
who repeats over and over in mock monotone–"Thank
you for your patience, thank you for your patience"
until we hear them just get real frustrated with
a chorus of bewildered "huh's" or mumbling
under their breath and a quick hang-up as
if they're the ones who have been violated
and how dare we–"honey would you mind
terribly turning on the cooking channel?"

The revolution has been postponed due to
the fact they have turned off their smartphones.

Fish & Wildlife

I used to work methadone in new bedford, massachusetts
right across from where melville used to shove off for his
brilliant nautical mad adventures called "moby dick marina"
and the dope addicts at 4 in the morning in the dark of winter
took their doses of liquid methadone and looking back remember
there was this kid who i was quite fond of (perhaps just reminded
me of myself at that age, innocent and mischievous, and couldn't
keep himself out of trouble) and somewhere in our rapport casually
expressed and mentioned and confessed that he felt like he hadn't
hit rock bottom yet, and honestly, still wanted to have his kicks,
and how good it still felt, and of course i validated him and told him
how much i appreciated him sharing and gave him my unconditional
support and somewhere within our rapport, as happened as well to be
petrified by the notion of prison felt the obligation through natural con-
sequences to have to explain how this might possibly be an option or
reality or just somehow, some way, more likely than not, become a slave
to the system, and whether trying to make a clinical or spiritual connection
or just the natural fluidity of conversation within this context i dropped
the biggie line "i got lawyers watching lawyers" and remember his reaction
where a grin just suddenly washed over his face and radiated and gave out
this natural chuckle of "that's so gangsta!" and have to admit couldn't agree
more and chimed in a little but then did clinically have to bring it back to topic
as not sure if he actually got it and explained all the possible risks; i really
did like this kid and do hope and pray he was one of them who made it.

Myths: 101 Easy Installments Of Pomp & Circumstance

#1

People find some of the most neurotic shit
to hold against you; funny i'm a neurotic
maybe that's what they hold against me?
hold me! hold me! used to be so damn
sociable and charming and hated to
leave family gatherings feeling at last
warm and comfy (looking back maybe
this is what it felt like to feel liberated
and free) in awful glossy avocado green
and gold wallpaper of 1970's kitchens
opaque sputtering vestibules which
appeared to separate the strange brutish
nihilistic outer world and the cozy safety
and security of the inner, those plush long bedroom
shag rugs of bone or ocean with beanbags and bunk
beds, sideyards which seemed to stretch on forever
into the deep shallow woods of backyards, which
always felt like an adventure of sorts of discovered
mica and undiscovered civilizations, cousins you
always fell in love with but not strange or incestuous
yet deep and passionate as felt unconditional and
kind and compassionate like the rich soil below
the suburban flowers softening up the sides of
split-levels, so as one can see always been
something of a sentimentalist, one might
even say a romantic and get so damn
sick when just constantly seem to find
the most neurotic shit to hold against you
when i'm about as neurotic as you can get

#2

Where's rhinebeck?
where's east rhinebeck?
i'm fascinated by places
like that by places i think
i've been to but really
haven't like my mother
picking up my jacket
as a kid after a lacrosse

match in high school as
left it right around that
private school where
they planted snipers
on the roof cuz a couple
of the daughters from that
cult the moonies went there
prefer grateful dead *europe '72*

#3

american haiku:

rocky balboa cracks an egg
anything is possible...
sun rises over philadelphia

#4

Dance committee showed up to my kid's class today
and told them no pda public displays of affection
and told them that boys couldn't dance with boys
and girls couldn't dance with girls and the distance
and how far that they had to dance from each other
and my wife told me it was the first time upon pick up
in the back of her car he expressed worry and concern

You realize some time in your midlife
looking back at lawyers and doctors
it's all really about bedside manner

#5

Wow falling asleep in front of the tv
i thought was something like the love
boat after sweet ejaculation relieving
all necessary burdens and pressure turned
out was in fact really casey hunt that smart
and nice and kind thoughtful newscaster
with the great smile from msnbc allowing
me to do anything to her and vice-versa
and such wonderful pillow talk got all
the way superimposed back to my first

gorgeous girlfriend from germany feeling
her stroke my five o'clock shadow in my
fisherman's sweater so young in her warm
basement in the shelter of glowing snow and
so in love and apparently need it so much now
one of those dreams full of lust and love like those
relationships the best kind and am like fifty years old

Bleary-eyed barely conscious hearing traces of giggling
and small talk you creep past the midnight beaming
christmas tree back to bed just like you did back then

#6

That whole absurd notion of men
going to topless bars together
getting drunk and howling
out loud has a real pathetic
and ridiculous quality to it
and pretty much turns me
off to the whole male gender
as opposed to that one beaten
defeated graying salesmen staggering
in solitary and sad in his tweed jacket
and tweed hat as if sitting back under
a whole other type of influence transfixed
entranced appearing to have some sort of
spiritual traumatic disassociative flashback

#7

Still picture imagine
that pale thin alabaster
skeleton body red pussy
quickly pulling that bra
back on as if somehow
embarrassed humiliated
in the middle of the dark
motel room in the middle
of the night in the middle
of nowhere and had no idea
how much i had fallen in love
with her wanted to make her mine

thin narrow breasts
like the strings of
a splintered harp in
the light of that dark
keyhole with fiery red
hair out of nowhere
whose fragile figure
felt something like
some forbidden guitar
left in the forgotten
corner to think she
was so shy and so hard
on herself and no one else
that i'd throw it all away for

#8

Please send
a close-up of
your lovely butt
of your saggies
of your profile
in the shower
with soap
in your eyes
going through
the same tired
lonely routine
and ritual not
sure whether
you want to
live or die
of your
pouting
and pride
of all your
suicide tries
due to an
impossible
to please
overbearing dad
of throwing your
hair up in a towel
getting out of
your bathrobe

dead or alive
of your fantasies
and nightmares
all of your reasons
not to get out of bed
in the morning
all of your reasons
not to go to sleep
in the evening
all of your reasons
not to be...in your
being of non-being
and these will be
your personal
bouts with
tourette's
insomnia
melan
cholia
obsessing
and demons
your own personal
obituary in no
particular order
and then would
love to meet
as always
beneath
the manhattan
bridge in the rain
on-the-run
like i met most
of them complete
and total strangers
sharing 40's from
brown paper bags
blackberry brandy
or a pint of orange
cool breeze mad
dog 40/40
living a life
of one-night
stands looking
forward to the future
gazing from my mad
midnight sweltering

summer window
on rivington
pleasantly forgotten
drained from living
watching the remains
of the carnival and all
the fragile and young
chinese gangster couples
returning home to hester

#9

Who gets to blow
the flip flagrant
flabbergast
dead fog
horn why
i'll be a
monkey's
don't give a
fuck who you
be trying to
keep me a
gainst my
own free
will and
volition

#10

All we dreamed of then
was oscar madison in his
soiled sweatshirt, catcher's
mitt and mets hat listening
to stick play that flute solo
from the gil scott heron
band *winter in america*
culture was dreaming
of him and felix best
friends looking up
at those crystal
skyscrapers scaling
the reservoir in central
park with all those levels

of patios battlements turrets
and spires between there
and the stars while at night
all the skyline turning into
a mad blissful twinkling high
ball cocktail drinking it all down

Mountain times bin
betrayed i must be
jesus, buckwheat
assassinated
that whole
summer
i spent
wandering
evenings
up & down
broadway
the upper
west side
only natives
from manhattan
know it's really
the best part
of town
west
end
rent-
con
troll
riverside
still $325
for a shoe
box studio
for off-
broadway
actors who
still haven't
made it
have made
it with a view
of the internal
organs spirit
& soul spilled
out on the
sidewalk

Joseph D. Reich

romantic
strolls
sometimes
even by
yourself
hudson
river blues
puerto rican
rican picnics
grant's tomb
& the pure
glistening
exquisite
silver
& gold
crystal
majestic
palisades
explorers
used to
stand on
top of
escaping
all the way
into the jungle
full of butter
flies & bugs
where teddy
roosevelt
as a boy
used to
blissfully
intellectual
determined
explore
to make
a name

#11

Dear Gertrude,

a man named mark twain
who goes by the name
of mark twain

who can't stand
the name of
mark twain
like the name
of mark twain
who goes by
the name
of the name
of the name
of mark twain

#12

All these very radical presses these days
i wish just one would return my e-mail
so i guess i am just confused to what
it means or what they are referring
to when they say radical as appear
just as aloof and indifferent as
the big time publishing houses
perhaps i'm just looking for something
as 'radical' as them returning my e-mails
or just a nice regular guy some kid i grew
up with i had something in common with
who simply returned my phone call and
said yeah sure he can hang out after school
and we explore the river and woods behind
the shopping center and grab a slice at sundown

#13

In the morning we see a tickertape running across the bottom of our screen
which tells us 'the rusty patch bumblebee has been put on the endangered
species list as has declined 67% over the last 20 years' while you imagine
the promiscuous voluptuous weathergirls going at it; the cuban bombshell
to die for going after the bleached blonde bimbo from the bible belt hollering
screeching tugging scratching going first after that long lustrous hair eyes
gorgeous shapes and forms and limbs flying all over the place while we
continue to keep an eye out for that monster storm hitting the sierra-nevadas
once again causing an avalanche ice belt belting the midwest and golf-sized
hail pelting parts of texas all somehow inspiring you to get out of your easy chair
and try that new coffee your wife picked up at the price chopper because claims
it has to be fancy-schmanzy because it once was $7.00 and went down to $3.50

#14

Sometime before the interview,
i want to be dennis hopper,
in that film blue velvet,
when he straps on,
that nitrous-oxide,
mask before he,
hooks up with,
isabella rosellini,
i want to be bugsy,
seagal taking off in,
my bi-plane before,
i check on my,
casinos in vegas,
ralph kramden hol,
low-ring to the moon,
alice! and her return,
ring my favor in hour,
brokedown palace,
with no malice just,
straightup compassion,
her own special version,
of a pu-pu platter and a,
punch spiked with acid,
and head back through,
cheyenne and sioux falls,
to find my pal in poulson,
montana (where inn the,
final call put the beer in,
the cup for the madmen),
from the whereabouts of,
the reservation to rescue,
him from arrest warrants,
we become thieves,
not by coincidence,
far more then any,
honest man...

#15

When you first met her
and courted her you
could do no wrong
and guess had that

infamous arrow
in your heart
and had the same
small talk and
cracked the
same jokes
and had the
same punchlines
now some time
after multiple
years of mar
ridge feels
like you're
pulling it
out back
wards
and slow
and pain
full and
damn
aged

No need to arrange
the roses on my grave
baby like the tears
of jesus in brooklyn
babylon bethlehem
like the graffiti of
delinquents of
past tenses

#16

Those days when there was no self-doubt
when all there was was doubt and took on
romantic challenges and adventures shuffling
miles through suburban blizzards just to be
with her in that smoky tavern on the river
through sacred and silent forests just to
spend all night with her in her midnight
basement like somehow suddenly catching
some eternal spirit in the moment and every
thing magically miraculously disappearing
and finally forgetting it all while all there was

was that moment…wow! what it is like to fall in
love for the very first time nothing ever quite like it

#17

The gigolo the romantic the killer the assassin…
on the back of a sleigh ride in the midnight moonlit mountain
just the sweet aroma of wax from cross-country skis leaning against fire

when he gets back to the tavern a beautiful blushing butter girl
silhouetted in the cavernous pub who also plays the role
of lover will serve him fresh warm rolls and brandy

she doesn't really care what he does for a living
just as long as a sense of safety & security
as both naturally fade off to dreaming

#18

Evenings, you used to drink
old coffee cans of iced tea
just to get to sleep and
fall on my filthy futon
on the floor on top
of the world in the
lower east side
getting those
visits every
night by
that black girl
in her white
nurse's
uniform
from yonkers
i introduced
her to whitman
and she introduced
me to god eventually
ending up writing me
postcards from san
francisco's tenderloin
telling me out there
how there were real bums
of which i knew a couple

who used to fall asleep
on the library lawn
beneath the stars
while everything good
and beautiful vanished
that summer like foghorns

#19

Drizzle pelting off pre-dawn window triggering memories and recollections
of spending summer weekends with best friend's family way out on the north
shore of long island think his dad was one of the attorney's for the stones and
eventually threw it all away or packed it all in as just remember him strolling
around the suburbs in his long white beard with his shaggy dog spending the
rest of his days like some bum just laying on his sofa in his sunroom listening
to the later beatles but now that i think about it and upon reflection must have
gotten fired because they truly were rivals hearing all those bootlegs they had
of mick jagger dissing them and remember those long summer weekends at
their deckhouse out in the dunes reeling in fish after fish after fish think it
was white fish but not sure so let's just say blues and there was some neighbor
next door you never saw and my friend and i after coming in off the sound
ripping off squash and dwarf watermelon and at dusk would try to catch
butterflies right before the sun went down so there i was with my friend
and his dad and his gorgeous radiant olive skin mom think she was native-
american and to die for just sitting back all bronzed around ten sharing
feasts in the fireflies on their outside porch of blues and wine and
summer squash and dwarf watermelon and i guess maybe that's
why sometimes memories and recollections are so important

#20

A brief run-on title something like the wingspan lifespan
(or how to live and die and survive) of the wild turkey
seeing him bopping his neck back and forth like
some fine brilliant motown jive from the 1970's
suddenly scampering past your dim grim
light-deprived suicidal window of winter like
some old yiddish slapstick vaudeville comedian
being chased by gestapo to the side of the road
not sure which way to go as these humans or assholes
all just seem to go way too fast for the conditions then
out of nowhere suddenly opens its wings and takes
off to the horizon as didn't know wild turkey could

fly based on past previous observed experience
of ambulation, range of motion, and disposition

#21

I used to fly those nice
ricepaper kites with my
hippie mom in the town
of mamaroneck (dig
the american indian
sound of that) along
the long island sound
when that convenient
flock of ducks would
always just show up
looking for their
matzoh & rugalech

content surviving off
fluff & peanut butter
on scorching porches

the eternal feint scent
of onion grass and being
enveloped by that waxy
swirling chimney smoke
at the close of seasons…

bluebirds & buddha drizzle

#22

Summer camp
was a cross
between
skimming stones
& a shot in the dark
that scratchy '35
coming through
the deep trees
at sundown
& moth-eaten
screen windows
of "taps" which

measured your
beating heart
& time on
earth

a trap door which was like some
sort of conduit to the imagination
and got you to the girl's side for
something secret and romantic

#23

With blotted sun barely peeking through
the morning fog you and your best friend
neighbor after a sleepover through dewy lawns
and fishing poles stretched in rat traps taking off
and peddling like mad through sleepy suburbs
and entering deep woods at the end of dead
ends to *carpenter's pond* to stand on top
of a waterfall all day to try and reel one in

Dew which had sprinkled it all
the whole universe and world
the curbs and gutters and
shutters and lattices
turning to a baking
hot day and returning
home with nothing left to say
but damn good conversation

#24

Later on somewhere in autumn
somewhere along the hudson
the wild giggling bridesmaids
looking like swans suddenly
taking off from the pond

#25

Mud was like a religion
and who ever came in
the most caked in it

after recess was
something of
a thief-prince

#26

Ricky Wiener's cocker
spaniel sniffing out stealing
and consuming his whole
stash out his sock drawer
ironically his dad a pretty
nice down to earth guy
and cut-throat prosecutor
from new york who loved
to nurse cigars just
like oscar madison
constantly getting
divorced and back
together again
that dog being
the eternal
punch line
for it all
for the mad
ness of it all
for the need to
self-medicate
and make
sense
of it all
we always
got home
screeching
around the
corner on
two wheels
the paper
boy really
not so
innocent
anymore
picking up
a route to
support
his habit

the romantic
delinquent
getting
chased
through
the syn
agogue
parking lot
by the cops
while getting
handcuffed
at the local
library pond
only to make
millions later
on selling
bonds
here comes
m. chagall
coming
in for
a crash
landing
soaring
with his
batwings
on-the-run
after just
robbed
the local
drug store
eating his
hot pretzel
and spitting
over suburb
ban fences
all about
numbing
the senses
all about
passion and
perseverance
leaving those
wings spread
eagle spread
open on the

front lawn'
having
forgotten
to pick
them up
at dusk
with a
baseball
mitt draped
over the mailbox

#27

Bury me in a GIANT con
verse sneaker box where
i used to live was a BUST
her Brown where they had
a Gigantic purple sneaker
i think like size 21
which felt bigger
than GOD where
you could fit Inn
all your problems
like that NEW york
Knickerbocker Marvin
Webster they called
The Human Eraser
who was eventually
discovered found
dead in a bathtub
in a TULSA motel
bedroom in the
Static of a full
MOON exactly
how i want to
be Discovered
and Remember

#28

I always loved the accent grave
it always seemed to just show
up out of nowhere when you
were feeling lonesome or

down on your luck like
some ancient grave
pagoda or steeple
and even though
you had no idea
in 7th grade french
what it represented or
how it would change
the pronunciation
or for that matter
your existence
it sure as heck
made you reflect
or consider or at
least think a little
what that gratuitous
geometric figure
was doing in
the middle
of nowhere

#29

I have fallen in love with water flowing through pipes in my wall
with my wife in the shower with the shadows of my son in the hall
with the flowers i want to poke in the winter vase of our kitchen sill
still looking out for deer moose caribou looking back to days of grade
school used to play this film over and over again for some reason
in science lab of the eskimo on the tundra of alaska and all they'd
holler over and over was caribou! caribou! and used to play this film
over and over again of caribou! caribou! remember seeing your wise
ass friends in the hall howling out loud caribou! caribou! coming back
on monday morning after spending a saturday evening playing strip
poker with a rival's girlfriend (who originally liked me and pitted us
against each other) and he and his buddies when he saw me chased
me all through the halls and when they caught up threatening to beat
me up but was able to charm them enough and think deep down inside
really liked me and let me go those last days of school smelling the stray
scent of marigolds in the muddy fields through the french class window
and knowing the summer was about to begin spending evenings pool
hopping with just the sound of me and my buddies like a bunch of
drunken slapstick madmen comediens traipsing in just our sandals
and underwear down dark suburban blocks where all you heard
were us idiot schmucks making jokes cracking-up sounding
a little bit like in the midst of the night caribou! caribou!

#30

How you used to just love to measure the rain
falling outside your window like some insane
mathematical equation and try to figure out
how far each raindrop fell from each other
just standing there solitary and observing
the wild waving storm or instead picture
the image of yourself swooning and swaying
and what you must look like in front of that
window all alone like your own private magritte

moses played by charlton heston
rupert pupkin by deniro

intense blissful stalkers
in one form or another

#31

Dear Ma,

please send playboys
and bit-o-honey's
camp is fine…

from,
joey

#32

Falling fast asleep in the back of her long 1970's
white oldsmobile after late-night performances
at *jones beach theater* where they'd literally
have the stage jutting right out into the ocean
this time yul brunner did play the king
in "the king and i" but went on forever
and couldn't quite follow and just
nodding-off and getting stuck in
bumpadabumpa which where you
were from was just a part of culture

#33

For world series
tickets you hear
your dad the dentist
mention–"i had manny
lean on mushkin…"

Looking back to that strange
leather medical chair just
sitting there in his office
in forest hills, queens high
on nitrous-oxide –hey is that
neil young rust never sleeps?
memories are tears and take-out
never ever always quite delivers
a cool album you had as a kid
you never listened to unrealistic
expectations impossible to reach
so instead became something
of a class-clown genius-thief
misunderstood underestimated
somewhere between ratso rizzo
ruenite and manishewitz joe d wasn't
quite as humble as you might very well think

Always find have more respect for those who kill themselves
than those who just hang around and make other's lives miserable…

#34

They keep on trying to shoot bulletholes through you
but what if you are so full of holes holed-down no fear
or hope like brokedown buddha holy-whole first time
you got off the bus in san francisco like a whole other
lifetime ago in the mission district been on the bus for
3 straight half-crazed days from the east coast day and
night running into each other running away every possible
and legitimate reason you could ever imagine when the
pennsylvania coalmines all of a sudden became chicago
butte montana sioux city cheyenne reno carson city feeling
your heart literally thumping leaping rattling over that woe
begone industrial oakland bay bridge suddenly seeing frisco
miraculously spring up out of the majestic glistening pacific
sparkling shimmering shuttering all silvery on the horizon

like some holy long-lost land of the eternal sun skyscrapers
of sacred steeples piercing the smoky matinee clouds after
being dead and kept down for so damn long you remember
that first feeling of brilliant bummed-out sun strange surreal
breezes awaking your ragged and rundown bones receptive
taking it all in and saving your soul heading headlong starving
sacred stoned being so far gone suddenly alive thriving no longer
scared anymore down tumbledown hills toward eddy 21 years old

#35

Mountains come up through the venetian blinds
to think out there they charge extra for views
to be around people you would never choose
to used to be able to dream somewhere
between the windmills and lighthouses
before you began a life of kleptomania

#36

Every morning that sun rises
over the mountain and seems
to seep right in & awaken my
heart & soul & reminds me
when i used to play hoop
all day in the lower east
side with no socks on
in my hightop converses
& run up & down the court
& this cool puerto rican kid
telling me & dropping the
knowledge how the sun
actually heals & provides
power & later on that day
when we were completely
drained invited me over to
his place in the projects
where he showed me his
22 kept hidden in a shoe
box simply for protection

#37

I remember spending some good decent downtime
down there down in costa rica on a black sand
beach in a bungalow after a breakup with a
maddening borderline woman and honestly
really didn't care whether i returned home dead
or alive. i remember during one misty morning
while walking down some dusty dirt road into
town through the banana and plantain trees
where all the young school girls peddled
to school and someone pointing out to me
on the beach how up in the palm trees there
was this whole grouping of vultures looking down
on the town but turned out they simply were minding
their own business and were nice and kind and ironically
if they only knew the bullshit and mind games and cut-throat
animal instincts of the tourists getting ready for their leisurely
activities how much more they seemed like vultures than these
poor creatures just looking for something good and decent to eat

#38

You sleepwalk through your kitchen
to a muted stella & stanley kuwolski
how he actually was quite humble
and not as primordial as they
really made him out to be
how we find out who are
the real phonies of society
some kind of psychological
role reversal of a higher
than holy hierarchy

#39

Insomnia
    is a throbbing stubbed toe…

to feel eternally lost forever at the luggage carousel
watching it go round & round & round & round
trying to find recognize pick up your baggage

#40

An egg salad sandwich
in a brown paper
lunch bag

sunrise sunset
was the school-
yard & cubbyhole.

we never went in
the woods where
we were recess heroes

#41

The life & times
of the forgotten
seahorse in all
its splendor
all its final
measure
meants
against
the pantry door
all that was offered
all that was taken
all the statistics
in the back of
that baseball
card the sub
conscious
and conscious
nest subtracted
by all
romance
and wishes
only thing
that mattered

#42

Listening to good ol'
michael mcdonald
from the doobie
brothers who
had a brilliant
beat and purr
cussion i im
agine myself
accepting all
these awards
waving hand
in the air
with bullets
flying every
where while
nodding-out
with tears
in my
eyes
not
giving
a shit
if they
get me
for some
reason
gave that
record
away to
that girl
who used
to live
across
the street
who once
hollered out
at me with
a girlfriend
afterschool
"i love you
joey! you're
gorgeous!"
and my
sister

cracking
up and
saying
apparently
there's
someone
out there
who likes
me slipping
in through
the screen
door heart
beating having
no idea or clue
and in many
ways ain't
that the best
way to really be?

#43

The glistening stars
through the dusty
closed blinds is
that pretty girl
sneaking a
peek in her
red pickup
driving by

#44

Those days those nights
when the best meals
were biscuits & gravy
at truck stops surviving
off thermoses of coffee
beneath the silhouette
of blownup mountains
and a sun going down
in a dusty dusk window
where real-life lonely
waitresses just as alone
and lonely as yourself

might try to pick
you up somewhere
between the pinball
and showers
the old timers
from the square dance
burnouts from the rodeo
what kind of shtetl
was this? what
kind of pogrom?
and your destination
was making it out
of the mountain
to the valley
to that brilliant
little stripmall
with the lit
general
store
to a town
where there
was never
a railroad
coal, silver
gold, dope

#45

There's a reason why
we turn drugged-out
and pass out in front
of that blazing yule
log and recommend
they have a yule
log night in and
night out dazed
drugged-out
god pulling
your vision
on the clothes
line under the stars

#46

You wake up to the silent tv to ol' time gangster movies to the beautiful
edward g. robinson and those doe-eyed cuties in their flapper hats at a
gangster wedding and are all in their dark suits throwing rice at the back
of a big black cadillac while he joyously rides off with her to the sunset
unaware there's a whole other car all stuffed with garrulous gangsters
looking to pay him back and gets him right in the heart as she vanishes
in the night and suddenly realize is not this a part of the partial history of
america while solemnly realize as well don't make movies out here anymore

The game show hosts and stuntmen are on strike…

#47

This generation bites
x, y, z you name it
jesus, jack kerouac
jim morrison died
for us and all we
got to show for it
are young kids
waiting all day
and night on
long lines at
the mall for their
techno-gadgets
can't even cross
the road without
looking down at
their smartphones
rock & roll and movies
don't even exist anymore
the politicians are a joke
nazis and reality show
stars are taking over
the white house
the porn stars
& head of exxon mobil
the new secretary of labor
who doesn't believe in
increasing minimum
wage & replacing all
his employees with
robots, our new

attorney general
with a proven track
record of venomous
bigotry & racism will
be our new leader
in race relations
the new head
of the department
of energy who forgot
the name of the department
during the last debates
the things we worship
the things we rape
and believe it or
not the exclusive
all-inclusive liberals
who won't let you
be a part of their
party as if you
were even asking?

#48

Tonight i was watching the college playoff championships
and couldn't help but notice the clemson quarterback
casually taking snaps and throws during warm-ups
with this little drone i swear perched right over his
shoulder and he seemed to be just fine with it like
this mini stainless-steel ufo just perched right there
in mid-air and then i suddenly realized what it triggered
which was that little green martian for no apparent reason
suddenly showing up in that cartoon *the flintstones* this pain
in the ass nudge anti-christ devil angel with something of
a sharp and quick english accent named kazoo i guess like
another sort of sidekick for fred to have to deal with and
always used to draw him into conflict and give him advice
and invade his privacy or tell him right from wrong but all
it constantly ended up doing in the long-run was getting fred
all pissed-off having to constantly explain himself to this little
pain in the ass superego martian now perched over his shoulder
and would just show up whenever he felt like it in the middle of
prehistoric times and not have to justify himself and suppose
what i was likewise most impressed by how this young black
quarterback just took it in stride and didn't appear to care at
all or wasn't distracted or bothered at all with this very strange

postmodern ufo drone just perched right there over his shoulder
like kazoo from the flintstones as for me in my opinion felt you're
always whether you like it or not having to justify yourself and
constantly having to make some sort of deal with the devil

#49

What is depression (situational or chemical) melancholia a term
which they say is a bit outdated but i believe very apropros and
very much dig and can relate to its mellifluous cadence and flow
feeling blue and down in the dumps and wanting to just cry out
for help while at the same time dropping to my knees and weeping
and wailing reason why i'm not going to take you up on your offer
of being your personal high-maintenance team member slave-servant
literally working $11.00/hr. with a whole ridiculous how-high-can-you-
jump mentality of bulletpoints you require make you want to just put a bullet
in your brain in/sane with a masters degree from *wurzweiler school of social
work* while in fact it's not so much the cliche of being overqualified but them
being underqualified in experience in instinct and intuition and the human
condition or for that matter disposition and bedside manner (moxie and
natural charm with guests and clients while trust me know how doting
and unnatural and contrived and overcompensating) and thus ironically
reverse-psychology, believe them to straight-up be an imposition for
this type of position cause mr. people person oi gavult! with short term
long term goals know that they just would not get it get me and seen it all

#50

Why is it that i always feel violated
when they start preaching jesus to me
and say he is the only way when they
don't know a single thing about me
and they were the ones who did
all that drinking and cheating?

#51

Why in all those really serious dramas
you always hear certain such lines like–
"i can live with myself" like in the grown
up world they set the bar or baseline
so low; how pathetic–"i can live

with myself" like playing some
starring role in a nightmare

#52

On the necessary nature
of 'good dreams'…their
symbols & representations
whether literal or archetypal
(even erotic) always provide
a sense of belief and belonging

#53

The wet bales of hay in the drizzle
which move past my window
heals all the brainwash from
the queen and her buffoon

#54

There should be one of those real true-blue dirt road
races where it's just husband and wife racing teams
screaming and hollering at each other and going
at it muck flying everywhere not just when they go
around the sharp turns or over the big bumps and
obstacles but curses and hurling hurtful words
never ending futile tit for tat glaring and paybacks
all sponsored by like mediators and divorce lawyers
and bail bondsmen and funeral parlors and the winner
won't necessarily be the one who crosses the finish
line first but who can put up with each others shit
all that he-said she-said pettiness and torturous
semantics and determined by who appears to
have absorbed the least damage and arrives
there in one half-crazed sane happily ever
after existential product and when that infamous
sportscaster chases them into the parking lot to get
their point-of-view or side of the story in their dark
sunglasses of avoidance will simply respond like their
normal everyday lack of communication 'no comment'
or 'ask him, they seem to think they know everything'
or the infamous obvious silent treatment for everyone

all around as this to me would be the ultimate all-american
dirt road race having absolutely nothing to do with who
crosses the finish line first but the name of the game
as always who is best at hiding the shame…

#55

Maybe i guess with all the hurt and pain and shame
these days just need more "price is right" in my life

#56

How to paint saints
how to paint shadows
how to paint criminals
how to paint martyrs
how to look back at paint-by-numbers
as a child and looking forward to the future
how to follow that streak of morning light bending
through window to the pot of gold at the end of the rainbow
how to fall in love with a bouquet of blooming dead flowers
how to build a red brick alley
how to describe the pigment of prisms of faux glass chandeliers
how to measure the plumes and puffs of piping train smoke
how to measure aromas and the past scents and triggers
of friends lovers and acquaintances you really miss
how to measure the difference between slouching
and when that kite reaches those high holy
heights where you can barely see it
how to no longer feel like a victim
how to see the nightmare in the dream
and the dream in the nightmare
how to not feel like an ex-con
convicted in the mirage
of a messed-up marriage
how to turn an upside down
frown back upside down
how to look proud stealing as a delinquent
how to not feel a constant sense of self-loathing
cuz they are the ones who are the petty thieves
not giving a damn who they are hurting
how to call people with the name of frank
how to call people with the name of charlene hemple

how to develop a temporary chemical dependency problem
how to hold off the phantoms with laughter and one-liners

#57

When i lie there on my death
bed and finally pass on
want it to be *the honey
mooner's* marathon
with ralph kramden
as think he really
was the greatest
and true-blue
misinterpreted
misunderstood
martyr of all time
yeah you got
jimmy stewart
and orson
but give
me that
paw
soul
ralph
cram
done
who
tried
so damn
hard some
thing my
wife ironically
said about me
right after our
honeymoon

#58

The lounge singer
gets himself ready
in front of the mirror
in his jumpsuit
of sequins
tasseled

white leather
boots and last
ditch hope romantic
suicidal splash of cologne
feeds a couple soda crackers
to his parrot who he taught
to swivel his hips and mimic
elvis' i'm all shook up and
jumps right onto that bus
at dusk which reads
beaverton and takes
his place with every
other mannequin
past the neat
and distinguished
post office bleary
eyed motels local
library of seductive
flirtatious high
school sluts
when escalators
of the movie
theater start
to take shape
and turn violet
in the evening
right around
the park and
broke down
donut shops
never quite
sure if he ever
really reaches
his destination
but isn't it all
about presence
and ambiance?

#59

The tick tock of steeples...

i told an inside joke to my sunflower
i plucked from my garden now planted

in my vase and for some strange reason whenever
i enter the room it sighs in a window of wilting foghorns

i send brilliant love letters from the belfries of throbbing lighthouses
flashing out of control for strangers just as lonesome as myself

#60

In the snowglobe
there's a shag rug
with him on his
deathbed dropping
a snowglobe going
"rosebud"
imagine
a home with
a whole room
full of snow
globes feeling
comforted
more safe
& secure
with dusty
blinds slightly
opened and
the snow
constanly
falling

#61

The tomboys with broken pinatas for souls
stalk the old dusty businessmen home
with wise ass grins of wisdom and
virgin marys locked down in cages

whole different version of the season
and a payback for the pervert

#62

How they used to give you all these dirty filthy looks
down in the downtown welfare hotel steam bath sauna area

and spending a whole life feeling cheated and taken advantage
would naturally snatch their canes out of their hands and beat them
over their heads with a lesson they'd never forget like a combination
between moe and the nuns and call me the provocateur but i'm not so
sure and if i could save one more poor soul with my knapsack all stuffed
with keats & shelley aldous huxley burroughs baudealire bukowski and
a couple phone numbers of much older women abandoned by their
salesmen husbands who picked me up at suburban movie theaters

Always made my quota and left them
fully-satisfied money back guarantee

#63

Unload me let me go after the weekend to the *burlington northern*
slipping and sprinting beneath the boxcars before it shrugged
and took off and would load up furniture, brass beds, grand
pianos and all all day long with ex-cons to make long hauls
from portland to seattle, exuberant, full of gusto, happy just
to have a job, barreling down, crawling, and hugging misty
mountainsides, valleys and gorges of those dew-dappled
towns separating the dark holy night and bleak milky
dawn, all very much worth it for someone so young
on my own, on-the-run, eventually, absurdly all for
those soulless yuppies you never saw who couldn't
care less if you got their dead or alive as long as there
wasn't a single scratch and then would toss you a tiny tip
how they got so rich experiencing the real life gross and
vulgar existential sensation and phenomena of 'nausea'

#64

(She gave up her winter coat to me
as could see i was cold and alone
like some holy mother for her son
young and handsome and simply
ducked into her truck and said
here put this on right in the middle
of the midnight of the mountains
and knew right at that moment
that that would last forever)

#65

The difference between jean-paul sartre from l'isle de paris
and albert camus from algiers is the consequence of
the reason and purpose of living (and being) and the
consequence of the reason and purpose of dying

#66

You wonder and imagine what rimbaud's mother's suburb
really looked like and how far it actually was from paris
or le sud de france when he constantly took off and ran
away through the steeples and carnivals and taverns of
the french countryside with his companion verlaines
his fine noble sister who sat by his death bedside
when gave up poetry at 21 years old and didn't show
much aptitude for the slave trade contracting syphilis
while only a generation later to be known as one of
the most visionary profound poets of his period

#67

Eating fresh sicilian pizza
beneath the lemon trees
of sicily by the sea.

on the promenade
windswept widows
and seductive sirens

pass you by
self-involved
in their roles

of what it
means to
live or die.

gay boys try to pick
you up on the beach
with rocks scribbled

in graffiti
which read–
"death to the mafia"

you head back
to the shutters
where later on

in the evening
you will catch
carousels blazing

#68

Acrobats with their vagabond children
stretch in the remnants of their lawn

there's nowhere to go but to vanish
into the wisps of fable and folklore

all is poverty-stricken but also rich at the center of
the core of passion of compassion of the imagination

a pale-blue snow powdering pines blossoming over the swollen
raging river where shadows and chimney smoke separate seasons

as an eternal mist hangs like a holy
purple blanket behind the steeples

one of the few things
truly sincerely reliable

big blue box-shaped victorians start to show through
the skeleton bone branches of the cedar in the hills

hitch hikers and bums add character to the town
while the drug addicts and the eccentric principal

with his seductive twin daughters
gather ritualistically at the diner

this evening they will be making
homemade whiskey and karaoke

having one hell of a good
time leaving it all behind...

#69

I want to see a *national geographic* special on the homosapien
of each breed & the growth & development of the wild animal
& how they arrived & survived & why they decided to migrate
to different lands & climates & geographic regions
of the natural derivation & development of language
& how there is a direct pattern & correlation (accents
& emphasis & cadences & rhthyms) to the nature
& configuration of the concrete lay of the land
of the erection of strange suburbs & those train lines
of locals & expresses to transport that faceless clan
of cookie-cutter commuters & an old black man
who stands behind his pushcart of liquor on the steamy
sweltering platform pouring them highballs & cocktails
to help ease the pain a little, escape reality & feed into the illusion
of the influence of specific medicinal drugs on certain cultures
such as tea & peyote & heroin & cocaina & marijuana & opium
of all the rivers & tributaries in the united states of america
& their rise & fall (& how global warming may have perhaps
affected the mississippi, the nile, the rhine, the amazon & ganges)
of all those original trade routes between continents & cultures
of the migration patterns of the runaway child who always seems
to end up somewhere between the phlebotomist & projectionist
of the philosopher (the explorer & hedonist) whose fate
always winds up behind the windy shutters of death row
of the cowboy & clown at the rodeo & the running of the bulls
of the cliff diver, of the flamenco dancer, of the cruel & brutal
& vulgar need & desire to sacrifice a freak at the carnival
of the role (of customs & routine & ritual) of superstition
in the most native & aborigines & advanced of cultures
of the growth & development of porno in both poor & simple
& elemental agrarian & highly-advanced industrialized societies
of the influence of the spy, of their childhood, of the development
(or lack there of) of their character & personality & how we naturally
rationalize & justify their behavior like the self-interest of human nature
of the derivation & true-blue role & purpose of the buffoon,
vaudeville, the mime, of the king's fool & court jester
of the gigolo & preacher's daughter who
deliver a whole litter of saints & criminals

#70

You ever break down in tears during the interview
with the whole clinical crew gathered around you
of the owner and ceo's and clinical director and
supervisors and fellow clinicians as you knew
more and had more experience than all them
put together as in providing insight and wisdom
and experience and an explanation suddenly
realize you were the exact same kid running
away as their clients and thus could not
only be sympathetic but also empathetic

When you leave sincerely hope you don't
get it 'cuz can clearly see they don't get it

#71

Eventually becoming a clinical therapist
you deal with all kinds of delusions
grandeur, conspiracy, persecution
and eventually find yourself to be
just as interested and connected
and ironically in some ways all
balances out and just as accurate
(in their effort to contribute and
not take things for granted) than
those who just come in to do their
day in and day out 'dysthymic'
whining, kvetching, and blaming
never once taking any responsibility

#72

One of my favorite kids working with
was that kid constantly running away
from home because his neglectful mom
cared to spend so much more time with
her new husband than him as if he didn't
even exist at all and had no idea the pain
and damage she had caused and ended
constantly getting in trouble with the law
knowing every shortcut and back street
in providence rhode island and ironically

ended up getting a job grooming the horses
in the police barracks as proved to exemplify
great carting and compassion while the cops
really dug him and used to joke with him
and made him feel so much more a sense of be-
longing and a part of than that infamous bio mom
could ever offer while can't even begin to speak of

#73

Most heroes are martyrs, not those saviors
who come a dime a dozen from a whole hell of a
lot of false advertising, self-promoting, and mixed messages

#74

The holidays have arrived in america
and you got all these mythological
heroes and sirens doing swan dives
and rising from what looks like the
blue grottos of the mediterannean
and it will all be right it will all be
alright if you just splash on one of
those archetypes called such things
like "mankind" or "guilty" you can
conveniently pick up at the counter
of *macy's* and will make everything...

#75

Used to bring the boys from group homes
to *yankee candle* in the providence mall
and very polite, docile, and well-mannered
patiently smelled each one of them as if
they provided a similar panacea of escape
of rebirth and redemption and might instantly
heal their existence, as they were removed
from their domiciles because were proven to be
'a danger to themselves or others' and for the most
part, just poor unfortunate victims of circumstance
having nothing to do with them stemming from some
really bad form of abuse or neglect, while ironically

all those awful mallwalkers and tourists were so much
more mean, gross, vulgar, cut-throats, and aggressive

#76

When i used to work at that bookstore out in soho with
my fellow freak & scholar from the badlands of brooklyn
for supper one of us would pick up duck in chinatown at a place
called *wing wong* and before we left would holler out something
real clever and histrionic like–"a blink in the eye of rah! a fling
with the wing!" then just fly out the door and take off vanishing
in the evening and dig in and appreciate each single bite in the
desolate bleak nothingness of methodical being and all these
creatures who would come in to try and torture us with their
lonesome and empty lives and project and superimpose all
their lies onto us with their mind games and body language
where we'd try to secretly get them out the door with a subtle
form of mockery until they'd get so confused and disoriented
or totally offended when they were the ones passive-aggressively
starting it and testing us like we were their servants there to do
their bidding and boy did they hate the sarcasm or indifference
when we didn't conform or play those roles of expected slavery;
sometimes if we even cared to make a connection might sincerely
ask them if they could be any kind of animal what would they be
and those not particularly swift would get instantly defensive and
offended as well and take off like a lion being chased by a gazelle

#77

Broken brittle bones get transported in the back of pickups
through the slick dangerous roads of mountains and if you
ever find your way out of them composed of smokehouses
meth labs nuclear plants radiotowers coyotes lumberjacks
drunk judges and madmen holed-down in log cabins with
chemical dependency problems and somehow find your
way home spooked by the ghosts of mortality through common
sense and survival settle down to drinking mugs of methadone
in front of the roaring fire with multiple girlfriends who all know
each other and seem fine with the set up as opposed to the
maddening institution of marriage made up of absurd futile
power-struggles of some kafkaesque-like illusion constantly
going back and forth in a hostile manner which never appears
to go anywhere trying frantically fastidiously to deconstruct
semantics from a ridiculous lifestyle so once more getting

back to that mad zen-buddhist scholar who'd just prefer to
avoid all the routines and rituals of damage and problems
reading paperback novels pleasantly contented sweeping
stars from the gutter, numb and naked chopping wood at
midnight then nodding-out in front of the fire with multiple
partners still wondering and trying to figure out why that
chinese buffet on the rambling raging river doesn't deliver

#78

I was that lone soldier who didn't exit the gigantic wooden horse of troy
as suffered from a case of narcolepsy and slept like a baby with a silly
grin on my face and arms wrapped around my musket. when they finally
went to clean him out and turned him upsidedown like cleaning shit from
a birdhouse i came tumbling out with that same silly grin, startled, dumb
founded gazing out to the pristine, sparkling kingdom smelling the scents
of roasted chestnuts and hot pretzels inquiring is this rio? reno? brooklyn?

#79

Part time housekeeper
needed (magic mountain)

I applied today for a position
to be a carrier pigeon…

#80

Religion
is the echo
of the earlobe
of the conch shell
pulled from the swells
of the ocean and put up
on display on the mantle

#81

All of them have become
blondes in america like
those rich divorcees left
over at the bar-mitzvah

#82

That whole image of putting slices of delicious pie
into one of those automated spinning carousels
at a diner for purposes of instant-gratification
and advertisement seems like the perfect
metaphor for culture and civilization
while how many in fact notice it
how many take it for granted

children lick their lips...

#83

The suburbs; what a weird way to not (exactly) exist

#84

Language only means something when you apply it
to an object but when it stands alone means absolutely
nothing at all; take for example the difference (and twist
and paradox) of its emotion and emphasis (and emptiness)
in constant repetition but its significance in periods
of primal need or even prayer during desperation

Obsessions are being stuck
between the too logical and illogical

#85

Original discoverer of the pearl, caviar, halvah
the boxcar diner and mob, language, love
lost, and the lineage of stars, at the end of
the boardwalk graffiti reads *shorty & pschyo*
and know you're not too far from home from
the fine line at the end of the world from the
ultra-orthodox scholar, acrobat and drug dealer

#86

How to make a malted
mock apple pie

heroin from
that pop up
pharmacy
in bed stuy

#87

A compact suddenly just starts to powder
its nose as her profile begins to crack

the mannequins on the subway cock their heads
like a sympathetic concerned dog for its master

elevator repairmen stroll into the gold
revolving doors with their doctors' bags

everyone making names for themselves
like those playing roles so far from the soul

#88

I am convinced that you can break down
practically every great blues to bee-bop
to coltrane to miles davis sketches of
spain to brilliant and keen gospel can
i get a witness to early stones rendition
to magician led zeppelin to marvin gaye's
street symphony mercy mercy me to the temptations
to the frantic mellifluous madness of shostkovitch
to rhapsody in blue to brahms chopin brahmin
bro man concerto #2 to straight-up hip-hop
'no such thing as half way crook...i made you
look' to nursery rhyme lost my partner what'a i do

#89

Everyone these days owns a glock as mickey mouse
pulls out his gun along with his mickey mouse ears
and gigantic, happy-go-lucky, slapdash feet before
he goes to sleep while the sunshine state is now deemed
and considered in the higher-than-holy terror/tory of a stand
your ground state if should happen to feel at all threatened
or life put in danger and you imagine him spraying some

rude and random idiot tourist lurking over him in shadows
decked-out in costume in a pool of blood in the battlements
of the magical kingdom while you ironically hear in the back-
ground–"it's a small world after all, it's a small world after all"

#90

That kid's song or myth or limerick–
"whoops johnny whoops johnny whoops
johnny johnny johnny whoops johnny
whoops johnny johnny johnny whoops"
in my opinion is one of the most telling
descriptions and configurations of one's
everyday swings of mood and emotion
or those infamous stages of human
growth and development with its
ebbs and flows and sometimes
even regression whose image
resembles that of a mountain
with its slopes and pinnacles
and sometimes they have
up there a radiotower and
hospitals and mansions
and mafia and madmen
and ghost stories and
sanctuaries and castles

#91

What was up with that myth or limerick or nursery thyme
'catch me if you can i'm the gingerbread man' cuz damn
if i was him would want to be caught by some fine cute
doe-eyed damsel all spooned and snuggled and put in
a total state of relaxation safety security satisfaction
and stimulation then reciprocate my sweet nothings
and philosophical nothingness by literally nibbling
off my ear biting off my head loosening limbs breath
of belly and licking all extremities leaving just my
ridiculous unnecessary brooding and worries and
a bed full of crumbs to remember me by on brilliant
bone-white sheets to live happily ever after and die

#92

To pass out
in my corn
flakes and
bananas
in the
windy
shutters
no different
than a new
day rising
to be found
lost & found
a new man
in a room
of staticy
ragtime

#93

I want my obituary to look
something like being stuck
in a telephone booth and
never quite getting out
caught in the act of
desperately trying
to rip off my suit
in a literal veritable
conflict between living
the life and a life of crime
someone apparently having
tried to rescue me or provide
some kind of support as can
see it slightly cracked on
the side and attached
with some twine is
a 40 of *ballantine*

#94

When all else fails i take the wife out for a scenic drive
through the backstreet cobblestone alleys with panoramic
views of the mountains burntdown nostalgic movie theaters

good greasy crab rangoon and three beautiful girls giggling
strolling home from school along the traintracks over the river in
their field hockey uniforms with their whole future ahead of them

#95

With dysfunctional families you start drinking earlier…
everything tastes better naked in front of the refrigerator

In the long-run, all the flowers go deaf blind and dumb

#96

Life has become a parable
i've grown wary of..

i'm waiting for that werewolf to leap
out of my dreams and serenade me

the old zamboni driver limps home

#97

I have this very strange fucked-up existential hypotheses
and theory that when we get older we suddenly somehow
turn 'inside-out' and our insides (the internal psyche) is left
just hanging there vulnerable, exposed to all those delusions
and denial all our guilt and conflict and sadness and madness
like the insides of a dream or nightmare and the only way
to get back is a whole other different form of set of images
of pleasant substitution and instant-gratification like some
palpable amplification of the senses such as art or literature
or the exposure to stimulating touch and sight and sound
the seasons the sea and mountains i guess my whole theory
hinging on the very elemental fundamental philosophy and
psychodynamics when we get older we become awfully
fragile and how all that repression or rather our defense
mechanisms coping and survival skills catch up to us

#98

One day just like noah's ark i'm gonna build myself
an enormous gigantic float whip out my hammers
my nails my levels my saws my masts my sails
and simply plunk it right down there in the middle
of my front lawn and then like some flaymboyant
ridiculous hero or forgotten god with my psychotic
million-dollar smile wave nonstop and out of control
at all of the commuters and humanity rushing by
i'll cover every holiday every memorial every
mental state of mind every sick and sadistic
war and battle be the prom queen and beauty
queen and drag queen and jerk and jock and
soldier be the sweetheart and spelling champ
and stud and scholar and when i'm perfectly
obsessively-compulsively sure and positive
i've finally covered it all am perfectly empty
and hollow and can't feel anything anymore
after maybe days months perhaps even years
climb off and slip right back in through my screen
door right back onto that dirty filthy futon on the floor
to my raw origins where it all began and i got my start

No one ever said it'd be a walk in the park...

#99

Put put put that part put put put that part
put put pout about the broken heart and
really trying hard just to somehow 'piece
it all back together again' that part about
feeling cursed by your fate & having just
paced yourself showing all this patience
& perseverance & haven't changed since
the age of being a babe & the early days
being a good & kind & caring individual
so in the end that part about being when
it's all beyond your control just becoming
a pleasant dope addict or pervert or real
family man or maturing wino that part about
transcendently spiritually deep down inside
never having changed as much as they tried

#100

How hard they tried the mean and the mediocre
to constantly stone you and what other choice
did you have but to become a man of wisdom
as you just crawl from keyhole to keyhole
barely hanging on toward a different phase
of life separating existence from the illusion
clawing grasping desperately trying to keep
and maintain the fleeting fragile spirit and soul

#101

So in the lone long-gone woebegone end
it's just a windswept town you feel most
comfortable in, maybe even a sense of
belonging where they won't hassle you
knowing exactly where the mist slips
down the mountain and steeples,
the creaking of bones, floorboards,
ghosts, rowboats clanking back & forth
in the seesaw night right below the moon
in the lapping lake house, lamenting past
girlfriends, love, tea & scones, imbibing
magnolia and planning your next run...

Eulogy In Ebonics

Don't get too close to them
makes you want to go ghost
used to drive past that skyline
of ours night in & night out
knew every street & avenue
& skyscraper by heart
your heart & soul
ripped wide open
open wide
lucid & lost
keen
street
wise
jigged
cut open
like not even
knowing it
violated
palpitating
ready
& romantic
it was them
who abandoned
you had absolutely
nothing to do with it
so fuck 'em!
& grew from
the wisdom
of phantoms
& rhythm
of rapping
as if a fist
flew out
the mouth
of a clown
& now
bobbing
& weaving
dodging
the illusion
knowing
the difference
between good
& bad & right

Joseph D. Reich

& wrong
& virtue
& sin…

Something Like Chocolate Milk & Grilled Cheese

i have felt turned off when i was supposed
to be turned on likewise turned on when
i was supposed to be turned off like kong
chased by the status-quo up the scenic
sooty sides of the empire state building
toward that flashing beaming red antenna
in the evening grasping at dreams always
just our of reach taking a flying wallenda like
quasimodo starry-eyed right into the misty lake
to meet my long-lost love through the keyhole

how the splintered forest smells
just like that pie stolen from the sill
on still and soulful nights like these.

A Declarative Question

Who asked Jesus to die for me?
I never asked to be born, torn
waiting on my rebirth as well.

I used to hustle a yellow taxi
(in NYC) graveyard shift
and remember night

in and night out
the back of the trucks
read–"Eat Fink Bread."

Fast Food

I remember delivering food for *Pizzeria Uno* in Manhattan
peddling my bicycle like mad racing those idiot cabdrivers
on literal missions from God not caring who they ran over
and showing up to desperate single women's apartments
who were like exhibitionists with multiple personality disorder
always conveniently dressed up in their towels or those towels
wrapped around their noggins casually wet and dripping as if
when you showed up hollered I'll be there in a second jumped
right in the shower and threw on their disguises getting themselves
ready for their act of seduction while always put you in instant
conflict like was I supposed to say something real quick and
clever like would you like me to help you off with that towel
and then throw down my warm bag of pizza and breadsticks
as all kind of felt like porn to me without the payoff while
any which way I was gonna get fucked in the long-run
so just gave them their salads and diet sodas and took
off as fast as I could through The West Village feeling
like an idiot frustrated just like them for the exact
same reason they had the need to jump in
the shower and throw on their towels.

A Bio Of Gertrude Stein & Alice B. Toklas

hide mirror, black cat, baguette...
(if don't have it can substitute for black bread)
to get to the essence of superstition or all the reasons
you didn't want to become a success; rain comes down
on the piano in the garden; you have lived a life of secret
trapdoors and keyholes to keep alive and nourish the mildewed
pungent soul; paint paint-by-number portraits of the girl next door
you add red wine to the ice like a blooming burnt down rollercoaster.

Scenic Route

she asked me to get a souvenir from the motel
and i brought home the venetian blinds

        (i told her she could always forget me by...)

Pain Scale

with insomnia you piss
into the dark bowl

thinking they're all just devils
trying to dampen your soul

those who have really suffered from melancholia
know it's all just simply trial and error far more
error than trial a trial of trial and error

bob marley said all you can do in the long run
after they try to silence you is write love songs

you start to sing the lovely love ballad–
i want you to straighten out by tomorrow

stand in the middle of your dark room naked

throw out your arms like chagall

and take off to the steeples

leaving just a simple letter–
what'ya gonna do?

Configurations

jesus got crucified
and still that night
the wives cleaned
the dishes while
they bowed their
heads and wept
and kept it all in
better to be
seen and
not heard
and that
night
religion
began

The Symbolism Of Nightmares

the muted coyote...
howling nutcracker
beneath the moon
every morning
my wife makes
up the bed
as if my ghost
lies beneath
the sheets
i walk past
thankful
snickering
like receiving
fresh clean clothing
all wrapped up neatly
in brown paper parcel
from the chinese laundry.

True (or false positive)

love weeps into the deepest
well of eternity which contains
memories and meaning and
uncontrollable sentimental
feelings which flood
intermittently from
the cracks of its
fragile being.

Please Follow Directions

After having that self-soothing hypnotic
conch shell to his ear for some time now
he realized it all came down to the sound
of that classic 70's funk song "she's a brick
hooo-use" not to dissimilar than the bum
looking up to the rainy sky and crying
out loud "don't know why there's
no stars up in the sky...sloo-py!"

Life Sometimes Like Just Having Survived A Stoning

the disco dancing of impoverished countries…
all real culture & civilization comes from the ghetto
wandering home from the $2 theater in hell's kitchen

                                    during the holidays
                        a survivor a stranger
                skinned-alive
                      in a city
                            you grew
                                  up & died.
                                ..

Sanctuary: how all language turns
to rhythm & cadences of the seasons

All reunions must be had
at *Odessa's* Polish diner
in The Lower East Side
with shots of whiskey
& combination platters
& the doors left open
for all the drug dealers
& thugs & madmen
& hustlers always
been something
of an extended
family always
been there
for me &
ending it all
with long warm
contemplative strolls
in winter below The Manhattan
Bridge at dusk on the sinking East River.

The Tomboy Class

The black & blue tomboys
along the side of the road
full of mad heart & soul
wild, out-of-control &
hope they suddenly stick
their thumbs out hitching &
you'll pick them up completely
ignoring me hooting & hollering
& whooping it up & will just drop
them off in one fell swoop always
meeting up with a whole other posse
of girls as if they're always hanging
out there at that exact spot exchanging
secrets & stories & seductions of boys
just like them kicked out of their homes

A whole herd of clowns, crying-out, acting-out
as how could you not help but to fall in love with that?

Joseph D. Reich

Please Beware…

If you should receive an e-mail from me
most likely i've been dead for some time
now or deep down in a diabetic coma
somewhere in the green mountains
as i have the worst doctors who
keep on ruling things out or
recommending things like
green tea leaves for things
chronic and concerning
or might just be our
getaway car (a whole
different kind of getaway)
humming outside our favorite
b & b most likely for purposes
of privacy, ambiance, and views
of the state of vermont as finally
discovered great indian in a shell
station believe it or not while also
beware my wife just loves to send
out pics on facebook her own version
no pun intended of being grounded in
reality, i.e. our basset hound waffles
from the woody allen film "sleeper"
and our mini long-haired dachshund
scout from "to kill a mockingbird…"
again if you should happen to receive
an e-mail from me or more likely spam
please alert facebook or my really poor
negligent nurse practitioner who has a
penchant or tendency to rule out or miss
diagnose or just not get back to me at all
although i've developed a wonderful rap
port with her team out of necessity and
hierarchy of nurses and secretaries

ps have a great weekend somewhere
between halloween and thanksgiving!

The Beginning And End Of That Film

how to reduce the baseline
        of your wife whimpering
                in the shower
    like a vase
        of wilted flowers
                the best showers
                      were in barcelona
            while the wild colorful
      parrots gathered up
on the telephone wires
at dusk
        all just desperately
               trying to make it like joe
                        buck taking off
      from that small dust
           bowl town
                in downtown texas
                      (ridiculously optimistic,
                            psychotic)
a tiny transistor radio
  permanently pressed
          to ear
    his transitional object
        which will keep him
            abreast of everything's
                that's happening
  (to late 60's man
        had it...)
              starving,
                isolated,
                    getting out
that glossy
postcard of
bright hope-
      full miraculous
      horizons to try
             and prove his baseline
                of functioning
                  and happiness
think when he got there
might have even ripped
it up and tossed it out
    his seedy hotel
        window like confetti

Joseph D. Reich

                    shirt off
                hanging holy
          from that porthole
                              into the anonymous
                                          madness
                                                of times
                                                    square

which proved to be
just as liberating
and out there.

How To Celebrate Holidays Alone
3,500 Miles Away From Home

Sometimes i was so broke
in portland, oregon would
donate my blood marrow
and stung a little more
(and paid a little more)
while dug the needle
in deeper a bit more
than regular blood
which just got me
only the regular
at *the china panda*
in stormy window
with a view
of the alley
at *the jack
london*
feeling
like a
ship
lost
out
at sea
that feeling
of feeling
both lost
& found
in the
midst
of nothing
feeling
my heart
palpitating
while putting
up the man
achings
for the
season
in a
town
acting
like a
city.

Joseph D. Reich

Blues Or That Song By Billy Joel

Swear to god gonna invent a service
where you can invite them over
just to croon and spoon you
beneath the moon that's all
lonely lunatics like you
ever really need to get
through "and i won't
see you anymore…"
as the stray waves
from the ocean stir
and throb and echo
and mellifluously rush
back and forth against
motel door which really
isn't a motel at all but an
open and vacant keyhole
to the soul and in the near
future when you get a couple
more dollars and are feeling
all low and down on yourself
or just plain lowdown like
charlton heston down on
his knees hollering on shore
actually got something to live
for–"no, i don't want her, i want her"
to croon and spoon beneath the moon.

Paying Ransom With House Money:
configurations, life-transitions & aphorisms

1

how many whore-baths
in my kitchen sink
do i have to take
to get me out
of my state?
life seems
one of those
long endless
boxcars that
just shows up
out of nowhere
slowly crawling
through the season
not sure where it starts
nor where it ends where
it came from nor destination

2

melancholy can come over you
from a situational depression or
a situation you feel you just can't
get out of or escape from or feel
like there's never ever any end
whether that be literal, existential,
spiritual, emotional, or psychological

(and thus, can see why it's often just the little
things eventually which push you over the edge)

3

may the bird bring her brush and bramble
looking for a safe and secure shelter to
build her nest in the gutters and crevices

of my home, and have no problem in the
long-run allowing me to live there as well

4

i think i liked it much better
when i was a virgin and some
thing of a romantic like the
madman salmon who swims
all the way upstream just
to meet its mate to mate
of course always keeping
eye open for the shadows
of that lurking grizzly
looking to make me
its prey all's fair and
unfair in love and war

5

it's crazy...i remember all the wise asses
i got into trouble with in my youth, while
in retrospect and truth they were the really
good ones i trusted with soul; not those
kiss asses simply just playing the role

6

you know that phenomenon where you just stand
in front of the refrigerator and search for something
and been staring at it for like a couple minutes or so?

apply that to your everyday life and
existence and being and reality…

7

i remember seeing that baby
bopping his head in the stroller
of his very young mother on that
warm summer's day in washington
square to "rage against the machine."
they say that babies instantly naturally
respond to music; to bee bop beats
and rhythm as it's an instinctive
trigger and parroting response
or extension to being in utero
and the motion of the womb.
thinking back to that image
of that infant leaned over
his stroller bopping his
head is still one of the
most 'moving' memories
and moments i ever remember

8

in social work school in washington heights, manhattan
she said she was going to set me up on a blind date with
a psychologist and was up for it, but not too ironic, or by
coincidence, just like human nature, didn't follow through
with any of this, both stood up by a false life and existence
of broken promises, damage, and betrayal and just that absurd
image of that billboard of the accu-weather team with plastic
smiles and a caption which read "the team you trust" who
i felt absolutely nothing for and felt so out of touch, would
lead me into the metropolis, but what'ya gonna do? and spent
my downtime contemplating in the warm autumn strolling over
the george washington coming to terms with being a stranger

9

coming into this world, this existence
our time here on earth, always felt
something like getting into a bar
with a fake id where ironically
always felt so much more

a feeling of valid/ation
and sense of identity

10

too much beauty may perversely
lead to a certain amount of brooding
(reflection and introspection) a sensation
or feeling of 'nausea' from a sense of profound
nihilism, state of blue, melancholy, or 'dysthymia'

11

who would even come up with such a surreal and sadistic expression
like 'pouring salt in the wound' like how do they spend their downtime?

like one of those sociopathic kids hanging kittens
or a little later on chasing down squirrels in cars
..

12

dostoevsky and bukowski both had killer smiles
cuz think they really knew what it was like to suffer

13

superstition comes with way too much time leftover
to try and figure out and decide why you made it or didn't make it
and all those ridiculous (and irrelevant) expectations which lead to that moment

14

i've always envied those people who have the ability to forget
as does feel a little bit like that concept of forgiveness
but too much of it criminal and complacent

15

froyd writ a whole holy book
called 'wit and its relation to the unconscious'
he should have writ another one about sarcasm

16

isn't it weird all that spirit and passion you still have
for that one moment (like a whole other lifetime ago)
of all those older women who used to flirt with you
at the stoplight returning home bronzed and handsome
after a full day of caddying during the summer for those
miserable wallstreeters and their soulless daughter-in-laws
confused, conflicted (about their reality and what they wanted
from mine) having no idea back then how much i really had to offer

17

fake aristocrats speak in opposites
self-absorbed thinking the world
revolves around them not having
much to say and it wasn't till i got
far away that i realized upon reflection
in childhood and adolescence i had the
need and compulsion to get into a hell
of a lot of trouble positive confrontation
and active rebellion with mad heart
and spirit didn't have a mean bone
in my body to sculpt some sort
of identity the puddles and play
ground and village at twilight...

18

i want to drive an ice cream truck
from coast to coast as some sort
of peace movement of freedom
i don't care who comes running
towards it madmen murderers

mistresses (at last finally
absolutely no judgments)
and just hand me their dollars
with their instant-gratification
smiles and i guarantee you
will make a real statement
and a better world to live in

19

there should be a movie theater
just for when it's overcast and
gray and one of those days
when those black and blue
clouds hang low and about
to break open and lightning
and thunder and all you hear
are the tremors leaving an
oasis of puddles while one
part of the theater devoted
purely just to romantics
and innocent first dates
and the other for lost souls
making-out looking to be reborn

you return home forgetting it all
also another type of wisdom…

20

rain pours in the brokedown mountain
crabapple trees have begun blooming

21

politics is the worst example of human nature
with its erratic behavior, sexual repression, self-
absorption, self-interest, need to control, subjugation,
take advantage, switch of allegiances, thrive off a herd

mentality, impulsive behavior, while at the same time
a single-minded, brutish, and cut-throat vindictiveness

22

gossip and rumors is the ode (the rationalization,
delusional behavior, prejudice, custom, routine
and ritual, and excuse) of the (self-absorbed
and abusive) obvious, mundane masses

23

the unreliable are so reliable at being unreliable
like the insincere act so sincere at being sincere

24

the most shocking things are things that don't
surprise you anymore, while ironically like
something of an existential whore, looking
for something shocking to trigger someone
or some moment, 'long-lost,' to save you
and make you feel safe & secure once more

25

these days fate or god or the spirit or good and bad luck
seems like one of those ridiculous asshole contractors
who makes all these offers and incapable of returning
a simple phone call and you're left abandoned all alone
wondering what you did to deserve this while ironically
as well left to feel guilty and like the criminal convicted
of a crime you know you did not commit; you ironically
once again see them with their lack of conviction, sin
cerity, and integrity as just a bunch of petty thieves

26

there is that infamous precipice just out of reach
of fear and trepidation but what develops even more
of a mythology and significance is its denial and
suppression, which takes on a certain kind of
high-expressed emotion and ambiguous nihilism

27

wow! think back to your life; about all
the bullshit advice you have been given
is there a definition for all that time
wasted or the opposite of wisdom?

28

having to explain you were just being ironic
seems to me to be one of the most absurd
and futile states of nihilism and loneliness

29

don't tempt fate...
wonder if anyone's ever said
like some mathematical proof of
law of opposites fate's tempting me!

30

our life is everything leftover somewhere between the dream and nightmare
in our dreams often find the nightmare while in our nightmare the dream
mortality is everything we mean, and more often than not, do not mean

31

most people with violent streaks in them (not the killers) are a cross
between moody and passionate romantics with erratic mood swings
and impulsive behavior often confused and misinterpreted as dangerous
and underestimated really with misplaced aggression and good intentions

32

i used to be so sympathetic full of passion and spirit
but then all the petals blew off the rose from the devil
deceit and bullshit betrayal of those creeping and
crawling through the shadows leaving the bare
skeleton of a stamen muted howling naked
and exposed simply a lone stranger to take
on the world they say nietzsche said thus
spoke zarathustra what doesn't kill you
makes you stronger i'm not so sure more
so a ghost (or shell of my former self)
from those cowards posing as friends
and family stoning you and becoming
the last one standing a warrior of wisdom in a
superficial kingdom of futile illusions and hypocrisies

33

i think if i could do one of those citizen's arrests
would throw the whole goddamn
world up against the wall

34

has anyone ever tried to impress themselves?
imagine that those who spend all their time
all their lives trying to impress or make an
impression? (i've met a couple of them
even felt sorry for them, and felt instantly
uncomfortable and bored in a second) even
hearing that phrase sounds stupid like the

(very cultured) audience at the movie theater
and those so-called pseudo-coward-scholars
who have to be the first ones to laugh because
believe they're smarter or get it more than others
those who prudishly cough every time something
sexual or sensual or has the implication of sex
and just feel like slapping them upside the head
and swear, really find to be totally appropriate
(there's another one of those words) as in fact
violating or invading my privacy and the exact
reason why i went there to escape society
feeling like just yelling "shut the fuck up!"
or "mind your own business!" as those
types always so busy trying to impress
or make one of those so-called impressions

35

in almost every truth lies contradictions pulled
from the polar opposites of its outer perimeters
by a certain centrifugal force of pure passion and
perseverance only to be delineated and illuminated
at its core nucleus; consider the origins and machinations
and functioning and configuration of birth and evolution
and the seasons, even the feeling and sensation of
liberation from a constant struggling and suffering;
the pure rush and release and explosion of pleasure
from the roles and resistance, conflict and pain of
living (the proof and path of the variables and elements
of a mathematical equation and scientific formula
to draw a clear and lucid and relevant conclusion)
ones dream state of literal and symbolic and archetypal
images while separating and also too fusing and bringing
together fantasy and reality with concrete truths from
apparent falsehoods and states of flux and confusion

36

i believe there is something which lies between
the subconscious, unconscious, and consciousness
(something spiritual, an active spirit, or metaphysical)
that they don't all just necessarily contain their own

separate categories and configurations, which get
triggered (or need a catalyst) by a specific event
or place or one of the senses, like the natural instinct
and pathway of the lexicon (the cadence and expression)
of language, which has its own thought pattern and natural
reactions (almost like magic) to the substance and meaning
of everything (the musical pattern of words) which came before
it, as another subject is just naturally brought up and discussed
from that preceding context (on a separate, yet similar plane in way of
mood and theme and feeling and 'being') without even being aware of it

37

did sigmund ever have a psychological theory
(existential and of redemption) based on some
parable or fable (or even story) of some younger
man having an intimate affair with a much older
woman on the same intellectual level and level of
experience and then much later on in his existence
coincidentally, literally on his last leg, his daughter
who he never knew he had, the doctor who saves
him touching on the principle and concept of kindness
and compassion having become the eternal existential
stranger; everyone having become strange to him (even
strange to himself) numb, disconnected, making no real
connection anymore to his psychosocial environment
and this one fleeting encounter and moment with this
fleeting stranger, who is also completely unaware of it
a strange and sacred, subconscious kindred spirit, bringing
about a certain amount of 'healing,' redemption, instant panacea

38

cultures, and individuals in that specific
culture transcendently internalize suffering,
prejudices, injustices, things historically,
cruelly, and brutishly done to them, and
genocide(s), whether inherent or empirically
and aesthetically picked up from generations
imbued and ingested into their psychological
and spiritual systems, traits and characteristics
(and collective unconscious, like osmosis, some

might even say darwinian) feeling these strange,
sensitive, nihilistic emotions, both of sympathy
and persecution, starting at very young ages

39

shame on all those liars in my life…
on all those who weren't quite honest
which is the worst kind and way too
many of them i'd care to count in my
life way too many lies when too many
men who lie so it's not so much that
they lie just that they're not quite honest
just that they're not quite exactly honest
are so honest at not quite exactly being
honest (which is the worst sort of non-
truth because it just simply drains you)
if you kind of get what i'm getting at
as this one is for you for all you liars
for all those who are not exactly quite

40

later on in life usually much later at night without even trying
they all seem to crawl out of the woodwork those lowlifes and
bastards of bullshit and betrayal could be a best friend or even
brother who share the exact same behavioral and characterological
patterns of the worst traits of 'humans' that of petty and trivial envy
and jealousy and would have and did give them the food off your
plate and shirt off your back and all you had was perseverance
and mad passion while turned out paradoxically the exact thing
they sensed and hated about you and turned to the weakest
of acts of axe of betrayal whether having no conflict about lying
and talking shit behind your back while interestingly ironically
always had their back imagine that for being unconditionally
kind and compassionate never giving up and having mad spirit
and they desert you i swear for the weakest and most insecure
of characteristics which only find out until much later through
experience and self-reflection and ridiculous repetitive coward
patterns (what wisdom teaches you which used to leave you per-
plexed and confused) really has absolutely nothing to do with you

41

it appears ironic and paradoxical
that those who always seem 'bent'
on quoting morals and ethics and
speak in absolutes or those things
passed down from generation
to generation are always the
first ones to break them

42

interesting such phrases and expressions
like–"it will be the death of me"' came from
places originally rather agreeable and comely

43

it's interesting, whenever i was the class clown
and they told me i was just hurting myself it always
seemed to come from those individuals who had hurt
me in the first place and why i was seeking a sense of self

44

all those people i was told who had good judgment
i always questioned for this exact selfsame reason
to the obscure need of why they had the necessity
to have good judgment and what really is good
judgment anyway, as takes on something of an
absurd phonetic and philosophical quality when
you repeat that selfsame statement and when
i finally did get to meet one of these so-called
people, really did not feel in any way, shape,
or form, instinctively, spiritually, or empirically
had good judgment, nor close to the amount
of experience or suffering you would need
to sincerely have that thing which they
claim like on a resume under the title of
responsibilities of having good judgment

45

worst part of betrayal is the actual act of betrayal
and the lack of (thoughtless) thought that appeared
to go (not go) into it like how language often betrays
its original (intention and) image and confounds and
confuses and puts into instant conflict the individual
receiving these impulsive words of mixed messages

46

i suppose one should not so much glamorize
their hardships as will find drowning in one's
sorrows a pretty hard ship to keep afloat
and to not take for granted there will
always be a lifeboat when you need
one while living a life and existence
merely with the will and desire to
survive and cope not really so much
as glamorous as was originally thunk

47

what humbles us and makes us mortal
is how quick we are to forget our
self-reflections and revelations
which so easily (if not vigilant
and often we are not) can
turn to a certain sort of self-
loathing, self-criminalization
or self-destructive behavior

the cognitive-behavioral task
and assignment is to just
simply consciously
try to remember

48

faith is that slim sliver of light
lying somewhere between
fate and mortality

49

has anyone ever stuck up one of those stuck-up
snobby tourists at an art gallery or museum exhibit
at the zoo or one of those very posh exclusive bed
& breakfasts and ski resorts where they treat the
natives like they don't even exist at all like slaves
and servants 'cause lord knows they sure as hell
deserve it and had it coming to them, and not
looking to give back 'in any way, shape, or form'
ironically acting all alienating and subjugating
and contaminating; those who really did all
the sacrificing and struggled and suffered
and were starving just to make a statement
or literal name for themselves; those who
just take and never give (back) and really
not positive or productive citizens in the
give and take process of kindness and
compassion (or for that matter even being
'human') real culture and civilization 101
would be–"this is a stick-up!" (waking
them up) and then perhaps can show that
on their smart phones (these cookie-cutter
clones looking to capture spirit and spontaneity
and real-time for a future later date) or when
used to have ceremonies and gather around
safe & secure showing off their home movies

50

certain people start becoming sleazy
at very young ages; can start as early
as literally 7,8,9, very single-minded
and opportunistic and wheely & dealy
and goal-oriented; they become of that
very exclusive and hoity-toity population
in the suburbs with the pool and very hard
working wives who happen to be accountants
2 or 3 children 'cause they can afford it and will
go on yearly vacations with them to the caribbean
or annual cruises and celebrate anniversaries
and will go through the routines and rituals
of religion for very much the selfsame reasons;
because of all of their things and items (whether
animated or inanimate) get good press and publicity

on facebook; and somehow have good reputations
(as if they inherited this as well, often by those who
wish they had what they had) at wedding and funerals
will even become one of those role models or father figures

51

those asshole alpha-males on their motorcycles
(kerouac referred to them as murdercycles)
pretending to act all aloof and indifferent
with their (a)pathetic pre-manufactured anger
and the exact same fake monochromatic
tough expressions as in america this loud
and obnoxious attention-seeking behavior
(really the absurd metaphor for 'might over
right') is supposed to represent some sort
of rebellion we are supposed to feel sympathy
for or making some sort of cultural statement
while ironically that pretty young graceful girl
in her sundress simply minding her own in the
community garden across the road means so
much more simply planting seeds doing everything
'humanly' possible just to make them blossom and grow

52

all great scholars eventually die and decompose
in the transcendent moment of some sudden
soulful image like a leaf pile planted on the corner

53

i like descarte's aphorism of existence
of "i think therefore i am" but i'd like
to take it one step further as ones ability
and potential to dream and feel hope
for the future no matter how inaccurate
or unrealistic; to realize it all comes from
the imagination and that our life and existence
dangles from the fragile, delicate precipice
and whim and strange illusion of something
of a vague, amorphous, romantic revelation

.

The Criminal Life

I. Behavioral Patterns

i'm the old man who sits on the edge of my bed who refuses to budge
who does make those marionettes and whose spirits run through them
i'm the loner who has returned home from the railroads from the dakotas
from old san franciscos i'm that girl who has been betrayed way too many
times before and instead of isolating and turning inwards all she can do is
move forwards onward inward christian soldier and teach them deep lessons
they've never been taught before i'm that boy who has turned away from guns
but turned towards gum and loves to twirl his baton in baton rouge louisiana
when they still had parades roaming through woolworths & magnolia that kid
who has recovered from tourettes and his addictions to opiates and now strolls
aimlessly through forests exploding fuck you! and blows smoke like a steaming
teapot i will be discovered having overdosed from bagel lox and cream cheese
with a strange slapstick smile they cannot rip off me somewhere between
the old country ocean and the crumbs of the static of schubert shostakovich
and sports and weather i'm like a cross between the fiddler coiled in paranoia
defensive guarded and that angel who finally breaks his shackles and flies in
disguise and spirals out of control over pre-holocaust europa somewhere be
tween fantasy and nightmare i get closer to my reality in crawl spaces on
the creaky steps of rear staircases in knotholes and keyholes and the nook
of your neck and shoulders in the spitting steam radiator of changing seasons
of the crooked tick-tock warped wide pine pumpkin floors of bed & breakfasts
welcoming in the lyrics of the self-soothing repetitive rhythms and hymns
of hypnotic maddening oceans and the frosty steamed-up lattices of winters
i'm that stranger who sits enraptured in the downpour of donut shops at the
end of the universe under the influence of sentimental and nostalgic triggers
i'm like felix unger who declares "feh!" (felix for short for sure you schlep!)
in oscar's startled dumbfounded face and steal really means it and leaves him
speechless i am the speaker of foreign languages that can never be translated
or comprehended like the nuances of thought patterns and premonitions
like all that comes after the vacant void of etcetera the elements before
they become elixirs the variables after the solution has been figured
how you figure pi (tastes so much better after it has been swiped from
windswept windowsills) while instead of eternally moving forwards going
in reverse in for the kill treading backwards somewhere towards its destin-
ation to the infinite absolute zero into the negative and a whole other realm
and dimension i am all the leftovers of a family together like the leftovers
from a buffet platter of shipwrecked phantoms leftover left on your rattling
night table in the most bottom foreign regions of portholes where the crew
never goes always trying to escape always on-the-run from all that deceptive
illusory and affected hardwired guilt and anger brainwashed for ages by a
buffoonish authority figure falling asleep horrified by the notion not sure

if the ferry is gonna make it and will i become a statistic new man victim
or simply forgotten (will wake up in the morning in the mourning cliffs
in the milky mist firmament of sicilia with the stud gigolo policemen
the miserable aristocratic women behind dolce vita sunglasses and
gargantuan dwarf morbidly-obese sons waddling from the belly
of the overstuffed ferry where dead dogs are passed-out in the heat
beneath the palms of the polizia in the strange suburbs of unknown
destinations where tourists are stoned by street urchins and proud
young radiant brides and grooms stroll through the cobblestone of
barking vicious dogs with fruit baskets mashed over their snouts
and sneering old hags cracking up from their slouching stoops)
there was a reason why i used to watch films over and over and
over again woody allen's annie hall and manhattan the graduate
midnight cowboy fanny & alexander and each time i did felt
like something of a rebirth then death and dreamed of being
reborn once again like some redemption from the crimes of man
i will accept my nobel prize like a ticking time bomb like marilyn
monroe taking chocolate and flowers and waving hysterically to
the crowd groucho in false nose mustache and bifocals putting
out punchlines with the ashes to his cigar oscar madison with
attention-deficit disorder and arrested stage of development still
smoking his stub staggering out in the morning in his bathrobe
with a hangover to pick up his paper to meet shakespeare and
sartre moliere underestimated only to find out i'm a mistaken identity
and that i have to return it matter of fact that i owe them and put me
on some payment plan my dear have i spoken too soon have i spoken
out of line baby i love you for how hard you try you are so much better
than all of them put together! i love you! i love you! like i loathe existence

II. Resemblances

i have often felt like a thief in my own existence
and only felt safe and comfortable as some sort
of transient stranger or traveler in a fleeting foreign
land which has been deemed dangerous. strangely
enough i always found i could sleep far better neither
knowing my near nor remote future showering in that
anonymous porthole of a steamed-up bathroom with
the echoes of a half-crazed, madman culture howling
'neath my sill and view of the misty miraculous mountains
majestically hovering over gorgeous, graceful, drop-dead
women married to killers and dictators; barely making it
back alive when the night crept in like a tightrope walker
with a death wish, and had something of a shy, self-effacing
grin which has only naturally convinced me i am not a criminal

and that much more of a compete individual (when the politics
and semantics of family tried to so unconvincingly, pathetically
prove i was not, shaking them all off with the simple shrug of
a shoulder, turning naturally, instinctively, spiritually inward)
i have thus, upon reflection and introspection, heretofore
in the circumstance of everyday living or for that matter
existing, frequently felt cursed by my own fate and
mortality, like the state of the poor, extinct buffalo
who was simply minding his own business, so brutishly
and indifferently swept off the plains and now replaced
by stripclubs and stripmalls and cathedrals and country
clubs, and in the soulless heart of it all, in the historic
district where they keep the libraries and law offices
and laugh tracks of bloodless bureaucrats and their
know-it-all bitches polishing plaques of nepotism
left trying to figure out and thinking up my
next hustle and scheme to get me back
to the blissful, maddening dream

III. An Excavation Of Situational Depression

we got stoned by evil relatives walking down
the aisle of our wedding giving each other
bloody kisses in the gutter by the river
with a pair of binoculars and poloroid
cameras slung around our necks; took
deep breaths and turned towards
the decadent strangers on the ferry
back to venice. they all eventually
came to resent us, these very serious
straight-faced, straight men not getting
our sense of humor, and ironically were
so much more insincere and insensitive
which suspiciously lead towards an active-
enmity and resentment, and some pathetic
act of jealousy. these days that line
that brando decried in *the godfather*
surely does seem appropriate and
can apply it to practically everything
'when have you ever invited me over
to your home for supper?' on my
deathbed i want to learn a new lan-
guage, while the dwarf in his top hat
finally reveals his disguise coyly giggling
by my film noire blinds letting in the light
of slaughterhouses and synagogues, as

my grades at last come in from gym class
i didn't finish and felt incomplete and guilty
in my dreams; everything i sincerely learned
and gave me wisdom and instincts came from
real-life thieves, hustlers, troubled girlfriends,
and black scholars, abandoned in the park.
where i'm from the parents ran away to the
circus, leaving their kids to have to fend for
themselves and develop very good etiquette
returning back on their weird excursions
in hot-air balloons, planes to peru to try
and rescue another relative taken hostage
or their all-inclusive cruises, while the kids had
to practice survival of the fittest in the very rough
and tough projects, developing stark independence,
a damn good imagination, perseverance, a personality
disorder, damage forever, and dreaming of the future

may heaven be something like the godfather
part II, the sequel, far better than the original

IV. Motown

they somehow have you perfectly stigmatized criminalized
scapegoated but trust me who are the convenient thieves
and criminals and could tell you stories and life lineages
that would blow your mind while how is it that i know
every soundtrack by heart up and down from top to
bottom of south pacific the sound of music rocky
which really is soulful really isn't that bad (not
too far off from mile's sketches of spain) last
tango in paris all of bach's concertos verdi's
operas strauss' schmaltzy waltzes schubert
schostokavitch yet they're the ones constantly
giving themselves self-promotions taking one
giant step for man from reformed to orthodox
keeping kosher claiming they must marry
a man with money getting divorced when
they were the ones who originally cornered
them and now want their freedom claiming
like living in a prison a reason why fiddler
on the roof constantly on-the-run had to
turn to opiates the song "the love i lost"
by that wholesome group from motown

V. Your Eyewitness News Team

these local bimbo
newscaster ladies
how do they get so happy?
i want to create some wax museum
dummy with those great big plastic
smiles, bleached blonde hair, and
padded brazzieres, and just
put them right in the corner
of my room for when i'm
feeling all down in the
dumps and blue during
episodes of insomnia
and can't wake up in
the morning like i guess
when i was a delinquent kid
growing up and we'd get all
drunk and pick up those orange
flashing cones from construction
sites and put it on top of our cars
and stop cars of beautiful girls and
stagger over drunken questioning
them and then leave them in our
rooms as some nostalgic remnant
but i guess i suppose that's a little
different but maybe really just isn't
just can't seem to get happy like that

VI. Insomniac Aphorisms

the nightmares of my guidance counselor...

why do all the sportscasters look like yul brunner?

of course you stand with insomnia your head deep in the refrigerator
with a knife bent over back all cutup like the segments of an orange...

that jewish girl who flashed me under my
porch in childhood remains with me forever...

the best thing about falling in love getting engaged and married
is you get to buy them bugs bunny slippers and looks so cute
in them in her bathrobe in that photo on our backyard porch
in that first bungalow we were in in bristol, rhode island...

still don't get or know why she doesn't want to get back
those arabic bellboys 'cuz we had to leave a day early from
quebec city and were so nice who worked so hard to please...

wife as of yet has still failed to save me am i kidding?
and i'm the leading man in some other classic drama?

one day i will revisit those other regions of andulacia...

get my hair cut again in sicily while the old men pretend
to break chairs over each other's heads on the corner...

the day lou reed died looked exactly like my nice jewish pals
growing up on the island both forced to go to the same anger
management due to parental connections and a whole hell
of a lot of spiritual, emotional, and psychological neglect...

i used to work at one of those video stores in the upper west side of nyc
and whenever the district manager would take off and leave i would take out
the movies on the mandated playlist like "honey i shrunk the kids" and when
ever he returned back with his secret briefcase would see a gigantic elvis
from "blue hawaii" or perhaps even something far more riskee maybe
with a little flesh beaming on the sidewalk and would be fuming...

the tourists and homosexuals used to love me...
(i'd tell them i'm straight but thanks anyway...)

interestingly used to be the exact same clientele
when worked the graveyard shift at *the pioneer
hotel* on the border of little italy and chinatown...

i used to love to shuffle home right around dawn
with the sky breaking open over the dewy rag mops
leaned up against the fire escape still with a crush on
that melancholic girl with the red hair while pee-wee
the night watchman and old merchant marine would
be having nostalgic meltdowns and howling at his post...

that expression man's best friend is surely one of the best...

VII. On The State & Nature Of Time

all of life & existence seems
something of a 'disassociative-fugue'

not knowing how you got there 7:01, 7:02...
dusk, the bewitching hour and no way home

VIII. Clinical Conclusions

The best part about the family get-together
and giving them a good send off was getting
out of my easy chair and going–"Look Erica!
I'm doing The Robot!" Had thought she was
in the kitchen and had already vanished
down the hall for a couple minutes or so
and after apparently having retained my
feces for the whole entire weekend usually
what traumatized kids do during periods
of crisis and agitation to try and control
the situation announced each one with
great pleasure one by one by one by one.
I imagined outside the bathroom window
her putting a Vermont McIntosh right on
top of my head by the barn and trying
to shoot it off even if it didn't work like
William Burroughs taking out his betrothed
and decided to just take off like I had done
so many times before after every one of
those ridiculous dysfunctional affairs into
the opaque overcast weather which strung
Halloween and the holidays together into
the ghetto which I feel I can always relate
to and always so much more welcome but
out here in North Country there aren't a whole
hell of a lot of ghettos so just headed towards
the weather and reminisced when we used
to spend weekends at *The Hollow Knoll Inn*
now apparently advertising a new gym and
reflected with a keen amount of insight
and wisdom and putting all the bullshit
in perspective in the parking lot of the
pharmacist while she got her flu shot
and thought man just needs enough
downtime to be left alone and not
be bothered with his melancholia

First time I remember in I don't know how long
just wanted to start the day off with a cold one

Proof #1

When they hit the road it did feel
something like the scene of a crime
with all the drama, betrayal and lies
where paradoxically have always felt
so much more comfortable and alive

All those triggers with a little less pressure
becoming a bit more numb, desensitized
defusing by their own will and volition

Proof #2

When they hit the road you find yourself showering
like Christopher Walken just let out of prison with
profoundly anguished silent expressions eyes shut
beneath the cascading water trying to cleanse and
wipe away the madness of his most recent reality;
you too were in there a veritable mistaken identity
working two jobs and simply asking them why
they were stopping me (matter of fact in America
if you ask such questions get a charge for 'resisting
arrest' can you imagine?) and ended up losing
both jobs due to the fact that couldn't explain
why I was harassed by police brutality
and went missing for a couple of days
straight getting a nice dose and taste
of injustice and shame and real-life
bullying in the might over right system
brutish society of my country 'tis a thee
put in a paddywagon originally in Chelsea
then transferred to Harlem then downtown
Tombs then similarly just like back then
living at the last stop at the end of the
boardwalk in Coney Island in the present
shave your head and beard just as focused
fixated liberated detail-oriented disassociating
that similar strange silence as if having entered
a whole other dimension due to another's abuse
and violation a new man handsome once again
as a natural ritual and routine representing your
newfound personal freedom but not quite the
same wondering if at that exact moment all
those super heroes you used to worship

were under the influence of some shit
taking a vacation or simply just
sleeping beneath the sea

You go to the leftovers and dream of wrapping
yourself up in that delicate baguette paper bag
and disappearing down river like baby Moses

Proof #3

For the true satirist (and poet and philosopher) he is always questioning
the believability (and credibility) of his audience like that kid in school
who can't keep himself out of trouble (or for that matter, detention).
One would be a bit ridiculous or obvious to call this attention-seeking
but rather testing the limits of his existence (whether literal, projecting,
imagined, or existential) and deconstructing those who came up with
such rigid, restrictive definitions. In essence, he has absolutely no
trust in any of them because all they have ever been are doubters
who gave him his start in the business so how could he take (or
even for that matter care) about any of their praise or criticism
as when it all comes down to it sounds exactly the same to him

'It is not appropriate not appropriate not appropriate not appropriate'
like the rhythm and cadence of civilization holding so much more
meaning and substance than language, like that rapid rattling train
suddenly showing up out of nowhere and disappearing into thin air

Proof #4

Wouldn't it be great to do one of those
surprise interventions on the whole
fucken abusive dysfunctional family
think guns and knives and gags and
blindfolds would have to be involved

(if looks could kill and
would kill the whole lot)

finally let the scapegoat go
from all the self-loathing
and brainwash...

Proof #5

I know I'm a sicko but there should be a Hallmark Card
for dead uncles for those family members who died way
too young tragically missing-in-action or just lost
somewhere down the line for no particular reason
who overdosed on heroin or maybe just didn't and
stopped showing up to bar-mitzvah's and weddings
because of bad publicity that favorite cousin of yours
you adored who I think got divorced or might just be
living on some Indian reservation with her second
husband somewhere in The Dakotas while just got
sick of family politics and living out on The Island

They all had such fine hearts and souls
one thing we always had in common…

Proof #6

The whole late Summer
and early Fall Erica kept
on tripping over pumpkins
camouflaged in the brush
of our garden like another
newborn discovered at our door
this adorable abused girl from
The Bronx accident-prone
a good sport who kept
on coming in with a
great big smile going–
"Look Joey! I found another"

Proof #7

In the middle of a jam
all your past girlfriends
show up to the mound
and start going at
it with each other.
You decide to yank
yourself as know
you don't have
a fighting chance
while the rest of

your friends and
support system
have gone back
to selling used cars

What happened to all our real heroes
whereas right there lies the true problem

Proof #8

As a kid he cornered me in the bathroom of *Taco Bell*
and demanded I unload my pockets full of razorblades
and candles and I claimed you divorced mom because
your male ego couldn't take that she wanted to become
a lawyer and defend the innocent on death row in Oklahoma

Where the buffalo once roamed is where
they're now holding psychotropic conventions

Proof #9

At my trial for arrested stage of development
I just stood there with a great big wise ass smirk
on my mug in front of an uptight rigid row of judges
with my tie I got bar-mitzvahed in and saw my
probation officer in (both situations not feeling
much like a man) yet was a simple walk in
the park like one of those clinical interviews
where I straight-up know my stuff and can
run circles around them retorting back at
almost every single comment they make
even ones they don't to try and trip you up
and welcome it as I got nothing better to do
with my downtime and then take off with the
bible and say o sorry forgot about that when
do you think I'll be hearing back pretty sure
I accomplished my task and passed with
flying colors as they watched me change
like a chameleon right in front of their eyes
becoming traumatized due to these kinds
of angst-ridden and existential ceremonies
which invites histrionics and lies at my trial
of trial and errors for all the necessary criteria
which might meet arrested stage of development

For example, I was that kid the parents forbade
their kids to see but always ended up charming
them leaving them all impressed and intrigued

Proof #10

The monkey is still getting shocked
in the laboratory and was just trying
to hand a bouquet of flowers to his
partner; you swim beneath the pipes
of the city trying to make a mad dash
for it below the old creaking vaudeville
floorboards and billboards of smiling
anchormen right around where
the foghorns and moon rises

Ponder that pretty and pouting
tomboy at this exact keen hour

Proof #11

Traveling carnival rattling through town
having forgotten its animals and clowns
oil trucks barreling into the broken down
mountain not giving a damn about human
life having been divorced one, two , three,
four times, tourette's not even a punch line

Proof #12

In the morning muted on TV I see these candidates
at the cheese factory shaking hands as if they know
each family intimately pretending as if they hang
out there on a daily basis and have ins with each
member at the cheese factory and with their very
down-to-earth body language and rapport and clothing
will make it better for their industry always for some
grassroots family-owned business which in my
opinion just doesn't really need it and not that
desperate and if they only knew how lucky...
then each candidate goes into a smear campaign
of why their rival won't be good for the creamery

I simply like Fall foliage and wonder where
their property is located and in what region

Proof #13

This is your favorite part of the season for reflecting
somewhere in the bare blaring beat light of your being
somewhere where you share the rest of your chickenbones
with the stray dogs who used to be so vicious and mean
and now treat you like something of a trusted companion
at the end of civilization on the crumbling shores of Red
Hook, Brooklyn where you used to contemplate, wonder

and try to get it all together hearing the docile solitary buoys soulfully
clanging together through the winter mouthing mantras to Lady Liberty
like not wanting to tell them what you discovered at the excavation
somewhere between the dinner theaters, bullfighting and coliseum

When those wild waterfalls on the side of the road start freezing
right around those secret forbidden inns set back in the lagoon
and trees and that burnt-out mansion with just as strange and
spooky a history on the border of virtue and sin with a whole
poverty-stricken town gathered around it which never quite
made it and followed in its footsteps when it decided to
pick up and leave with similar remnants and scenes which
transcendently became the bizarre beacon of your being...

Proof #14

To sometimes
calm yourself
you think of
those old
Greeks
going
down
on
those
down
trodden
donkeys
at dusk
to the
sea

No Safe Place To Even Kill Yourself Anymore

I.

They peek through the lace leaves
                 of the deep trees of the forest
& just think of laying out condominium
        complexes, country clubs, panoramic
golf ranges...
        doesn't even cross their minds
anymore, the change of seasons
        how the lagoon
the moon
   looked exactly
      like this the first day
              of evolution

II.

The lovely lugubrious creatures...
                 that dainty long-legged, long-necked
lady egret who gets startled
            by the most sudden, subtle & fragile of things
& takes off, wings flapping madly, majestically
         through the ancient, hanging, cedar ivy
the Jesus Christ lizards
        walking on water, waltzing like madmen
                across ricepaper lilypads
the ping-pong volley
          deep, guttural, rhythmic croaking
going back & forth
        like the pillow talk
of midnight tadpoles
      with secret riddles & punchlines
that only time can comprehend
              the miraculous sweep of the breeze
which heals everything
         & its simple scattered symphonies
were exactly this intense, this sweet
                when time originally began

III.

Yet due to the exact copycat
        mean & aggressive ways of man

(what they compulsively like to refer
      to as "competition")
still gather around
     over your late-night, local cable station
like ignorant & oppressed domestic animals
       with agendas of anger & alienation
why/need about zoning boards, terror/tories & neighbors
    how the 'neighings' disturbing the peace
& feeling like something of a form of murder
      when returning home after
a full day of going in for the kill & cut-throat quotas
    & those the most successful
those who show the least contrition

IV.

  It is also of interest to note
how that clap of thunder
  brings home the bones
of the lone romantic
  which of course as always
historically, spiritually, transcendentally
       goes without notice
referred to in passing
  "as look what the cat dragged in"
by that whole swarm of pseudo-scholars & wannabe's
    who haven't seen a thing
unaware you know
     exactly where they haven't been
& how much more obvious & filthy
       exchanging virtue for sin

V.

What the wind, what wandering all by your lonesome
       in cities of cobblestone did to you
the same ghost women, the same black men
       blowing the blues
how picking up a single transistor from a pawnshop
       on *Toulouse*
meant the world to you
   listening to ragtime & Jimmy Rogers
yodeling through scratchy record
       static on this side & that side
of the Mississippi, healing your melancholy

Joseph D. Reich

     when you had absolutely no one to turn to
on starving Sundays
  & the shivering change of seasons

VI.

Dreaming of where you were from way up north,
      Harlem-Valley Psychiatric
the last stop on the metro-north
    not too far from *The Red Rooster*
where the pot of gold at the end of the rainbow
    was cheeseburgers, onion rings & miniature golf
while a little further up
   in the blessed land of The Berkshires
had one-night stands, summer affairs
    with gorgeous smart red heads
on the lake laying out future plans
     silhouetted, naked in front of
sweltering 3 a.m. windows
   with fans slowly stuttering in sills
developing relationships
   with nocturnal creatures stirring in the wilderness

VII.

A whole summer of
  whiskey, marijuana,
sex & arrest warrants
  (cheddar & potato bread
from that general store
   in the forest)
'cuz just like Brando
   never cared to check your mailbox
& was that crazy, conspiratorial
     girl across the hall
(a whole long historical rap sheet & all)
   who got jealous
'cuz you didn't choose her
   & was just I swear
trying to mind your own
   & find a place to rest your bones
only to discover
   that "home"
is illusory, fleeting & ephemeral
    in the moment

VIII.

How that sudden scent
        of swirling chimneys
                got you back to reality
back on-the-run
      to the city
with your transitory, skeletal being
              in the radiant anonymity
of romantic
      madman Delancey
contemplating fallen
          blazing leaves
in the brilliant bleak
        dusk of the empty pool on Pitt St.

IX.

That black ex-nun from Yonkers
          & Puerto Rican angel from Brooklyn
both with drinking problems
    'on-the-run' from themselves
all of us involved in a strange
        intellectual
     sensuous
        manifest-destiny
her sending postcards
        from The Mission District
in San Francisco
     & telling me this is where
the real bums were
        was translating the bible
into calligraphy
           while I introduced her, awestruck,
to 'Leaves'
    just as brilliant & redemptive by Whitman

X.

All too keenly aware, upon reflection
        coincidence rarely comes by coincidence
                if know & comprehend the spirits
& sensitive patterns of the universe
      how the hollow echo of all these elements
          time, patience, memories, mysteries, moments

                  somewhere between the ecosystem & evolution
magically, sentimentally, takes on
            a more holy & haunted significance
like the skimming of a stone over
                some still sacred mirrored lake surface
& each leap representing ages
            in the scope of the vast brooding blissful unknown

XI.

How we get naturally, proportionately lonelier
                    when we get older
when places which used to be sanctuaries
                    turn to triggers
when dreams turn to nightmares
            even certain parts of the home
you prefer to be in
      to fall asleep, to wake up in
when you used to be this adventurous, curious, mischievous
                            creature
now a little slower, a little less instinctive
                  blindly following around
like a dog some authority figure
        who used to never pay you attention
as if sensing now your own mortality
            & make sure like some custom
or ritual to go right back
        day in & day out
            to that exact same spot in front of the fire

XII.

Everything from the wild
    the moon, the midnight, the mountains
has rubbed off on you
        which scares the bejesus out of them
(makes them resentful & defensive)
               & gives you strength & wisdom
something not in the original plan
        of the conquering kingdom

XIII.

As believe they exist
   & what makes them men

        when they show up
                in their hard hats,
                        walkie-talkies,
                              orange cone,
                                      blueprints
with those f-35 bombers
                        or *Blue Angels*
doing nosedives
                over the stripmall
triggering your post-traumatic stress disorder
                                  making your skin crawl
& wanting to crawl right back in the hole

XIV.

To know your only true-blue
                soulmates & companions
the only ones you can sincerely
                        rely on
are the shoeless bucktooth
                        Darwinian gods
who have lasted forever
                in the swamp
going back & forth
                like loving mothers
on a thankless, futile
           'Myth of Sysiphus' mission
& built their mansions
                through hard work & perseverance
 out of sticks & mud.
                      with the faith & will to move on.

Pool Rules: The Life-Cycle (from a cognitive-behavioral perspective) Or A Darwinian Comparison Between The Animal Kingdom And Homo Sapien

An Abstract:

[How much the structure of the dream resembles the physiological makeup of the cell, while at its core, is the subconscious/self-image; between that and the periphery, the active/surreal being (in good dreams of liberation, fantasy/instant gratification, in nightmares, stagnation/isolation) and the outer boundary, how one acts-out, or reactively present themselves, primitively represented/manifested in their psychosocial environment]

1. Been starting to spend some of my summer at the pool
and funny am like 40 years older and the same mean girls
in sunglasses, hell-bent on playing the same games, acting
angry and alienating, like you've violated them or their sister
or some secret code of ethics (what it really comes down to
most likely are frigid prudes with some sort of sexual disorder)
and ironically the exact same mean bitches for no reason in
particular, no longer really a challenge, as in a cognitively-
distorted way think the world still revolves around them

2. The jealous lifeguards staring you down
(insecure and fragile, angry and hostile)
instantly giving themselves away
like they did so long ago

3. The wannabe white trash (sarcastic who have never left
the boundaries of their existence) and always want to start
something up and still apparently haven't done much with
their lives or as Kerouac alluded to you go into a white bar
and they always want to fight, but enter a black one, mind
their own, modest and humble and just want to groove and
get down and have a good time and be kind and welcoming

4. The glossy high school girls spreading their anatomies
(for all to see) baring their flesh like some fish on a platter
always in their look-a-like clusters of you can look but can
not touch superhero sets of 3 ready to take over the world

5. College girls to die for who any man or husband would throw
it all way for and become an instant breath of fresh air just like
the low-lying iridescent clouds over the surrounding mountains
who will eventually become fantasy and masturbatory and really
no one doing their job, just this cat & mouse Cleopatra seduction

for immature hard-up boys hoping to get laid with their health club
muscles, instantly getting ignored and the rest of them dads who
they put their smoke & mirror Madonna/Whore signals out for

6. Some flat-chested single female in her black one-piece
standing at the end of the lanes very meticulously pulling
on her swimming cap, self-conscious and demure, and
when she returns home alone at dusk will most likely
go through the exact same similar routine and ritual

7. Some lost lone beaten defeated solitary male with a pasty blue gray
complexion probably some sort of actuary-accountant-insurance man
who hobbles over to the pool and then vanishes in thin air and
never seen from or heard from again like a fish tossed back in

8. Desperate and dangerous divorcees (who haven't gotten it in ages...)
having absolutely no problem, no qualm or conflict with being promiscuous
and starting scandals with best friend's husbands who work with their child

9. Mounds and mounds of flesh with no shape or form
and faded, stretched-out tattoos (supposed to be all taboo)
put in specific seductive places made to try and turn you on

10. The queen who acts like a princess
in her sunglasses way up on her throne

11 Greatest action & adventure, those kids climbing the stairs
to the top of the ladder and taking courageous cliff-dive, swan-
dive leaps-of-faith and landing in strange awkward dog-like belly
flops of course being gluttons sucking up the pain and humiliation
and almost in the same state of flux and motion and literal 'fell
swoop' scampering right back up again to get more abuse

12. With your eyes closed you take in
low-lying clouds and wind blowing
through the surrounding mountains

13. The speaker calls everybody back in from
Family Swim and all that's left is the thin ripples
self-soothing, clandestine, vanishing to the season

14. You stroll home contemplative within the distant
claps of thunder, wondering if it was all worth it...
What is it that will make you finally feel contented?

Joseph D. Reich

The Life & Times Of Bazooka Joe

With their own insecurities they accuse you
of cheating 'cuz you can see right through them
and already know exactly what they're gonna say
not in the obvious cliche domestic quarrel way and
say to yourself what ya gonna do I always been that

way and sick of feeling like a criminal and guilty because
they underestimate you and was just born like this (who are
the real fucken jealous misfits!) reason why they invented
for the innocent 'can I get a witness' and knew at a very
young age was gonna live a life feeling eternally lonely.

You grew up in the alley which connected the city to the sea
this is how you contemplated the seasons like a stray dog
relying on its instincts, starving and keen, spending days
wasted, washed away in the maddening church bells
and wailing wild seagulls behind the cathedral

like some trapdoor
separating all things
mortal from mystical
and time immemorial

the geek in the belfry who kept
making that staticy record skip
conflicted between fate and risk
and being a romantic or fatalist

like some blind date who deliberately
doesn't show up or swingers who
give you the wrong address.

You read your fortune
by the dope addicts
shooting up on park
benches by the river

Eccentric old ladies in their teatime dresses
taking tea around the teatable giggling
and acting giddy in the trampoline

afro of a weeping black man
sulking in his jump
suit of sequins.

This time elegies are given by the dead
who claim they just got nothing left
to live for and more monotone than
the machinations of a mechanical
message machine repeating
all it is is sadness and suffering
so constantly must be changing.

There's a welcome home ceremony
given for the hustler who gets out
on good behavior with a banner
swinging from the fire escape
where he originally started.

After all your superstition
disguised for prayer you find
yourself in bed with insomnia
and tourette's going fuck 'em!

finally departing the radiant dusty plains
of tombstones where all great punchlines
came from seeing the cows at their trough
and can't help but give them a furtive grin.

They accuse you of being unpatriotic 'cuz
your ambidextrous and got your hand on
your appendix completely unaware you
got your palm on your pistol and always
been a rebel just don't know any different

like a couple gorgeous cherubic kids hysterical
in the back seat of a car declaring "I will destroy
you!" then giving each other first kisses while
lying against the dewy lawn beneath the stars.

Always saw yourself as something of a romantic
while that splintered Horse of Troy instead of being
filled with killers, all stuffed with fiddlers, but
guess that was the whole gist of it cruel hoax
of civilization leaving you eternally stranded

dreaming of some phase to phase away that phase
or some other phase patiently waiting in the wings
scooping this one up and stealing away like Chaplin
in factory rags, cap and cane waddling away offstage

Joseph D. Reich

dreaming of that paradise just past the ghetto
right around the corner where no one knows
you falling asleep with a slapstick smile
like Darwin, Dagwood, Darren from Be-
witched Cary Grant from *Catch a Thief.*

You welcome all break-ins
all metamorphoses
which might make
you a better man

The weather the only thing
keeping you together, to know
the helicopters will be flying low
following the railroad from Lake
Placid to South Burlington; will
be setting the beartraps so don't
let your dog swim in the riverbanks

possible mountainflakes
always a certain type
of awakening always
a certain type of magical
and metaphysical break…

Something Like Radio Or The Hx Of The Black
Dope Addict Floorwaxer Floating Around The Foyer

i sit back
      numb,
          relaxed,
              ecstatic
                  in my easy chair

  gazing out
        in the very
                early morning

at the first snows
            falling,
                swirling,
                    blowing
                        all around

  the bare purple mountains
                a slight light
                      streaming from the overcast sky
     cracked open
         like an egg overeasy

            the glazed telephone wires...

mists seeping over the pinnacle
            & steeples
          & chandeliers

            of the mountain

                  & man tell you
                      nothing feels better
                          reflective, introspective
    then gradually somehow
            moves up
                to the great bright dome above

which opens my heart
      & think this must be like
            what heaven is
                hell i've tried every other option

Joseph D. Reich

                                        & think of sending my wife & kid
                        on a cruise
            they deserve it.

Baileys Irish

I couldn't stand going to college in The Deep South
a matter fact loved the atmosphere and ambiance
and the ghosts and madwomen and what felt like
other strange spirits; the historic rattling streetcar
which languidly took you back and forth to campus
deep sweet pungent scents of Magnolia and Crepe
Myrtle all abound, the hanging Spanish Moss and
mausoleums, but ironically couldn't stand the students
these rich obnoxious brats from The Northeast mostly
The Island arrogantly driving around in the cars their
parents had bought them, having no respect for the
environment around them and this mood and mentality
actually led to me isolating and feeling situationally
depressed never going to class surviving off apple
Pop Tarts and Coors Beer and reading philosophy
and classics off other kids syllabuses I guess
making me something of a self-educated and
independent thinker and whenever I was able
to get away and head back home for the holidays
we used to see these advertisements in the airports
and on the trains in Grand Central Station which made
me feel even more alienated of these very clean-cut
greedy yuppies and up and coming climbers all
ecstatic and gathered around their *Baileys Irish*
with these really plastic, elastic, pasted-on, ear
to ear smiles and my friends and I would always
try to imitate them while waiting for our luggage
to show up on the carousels taking long endless strolls
of contemplation all by my lonesome through the winter
wonderland of the suburbs getting picked up by this gorgeous
frauline pretending to ask for directions meeting your first radiant
girlfriend from The Rhineland spending romantic nights in smoky taverns
and the snow building up in the windowsills of her basement waking up wasted
to Jimmy Stewart leaping off frozen bridges in periods of desperation then redemption.

Joseph D. Reich

Parts Of Speech

{all of it was that but most of it wasn't}

i know i'm a glutton but when i was on my own and having nowhere to go
maybe trying to pick up some cute girl over a frappuccino i used to always
love seeing those book signings at like *barne's & noble* where the author
was just sitting at some really long table all alone and down on his luck
like jesus' last supper and no one shows up and left all by his lonesome
just starts naturally being really tough on himself me thinking so surreal
and if it was me wouldn't care less and cut myself and bleed to death

me not being much of a savior as just couldn't deal with the pressure…

{meanings}

i always hated words like "anomaly" like 'he/she is an anomaly'
as people are always trying to define each other or ascribe some
concrete factor or measurement to the equation while most likely
just trying to function get along and figure out the purpose to their
existence or in most cases just trying to prove something they isn't

{anti-meaning}

like those who try to get you with the constant guilt in the subtle vicious abuse
cycle of claiming how much they are constantly worrying about you as first
instinct is mind your business! while really, deep down inside, most likely
want to control you (not receptive pretty rigid) treat you like a possession

{the law of opposites}

came into this world by coincidence
by mistake by a form of rape
in the morning you reach
for the *land-o-lakes*
in the refrigerator
as that gigantic bear
shows up to your window
for reasons far more existential
than survival the fog makes you
feel alive gets you closer to god

"in the next hour we'll hear from
stravinsky, verdi, and bach..."

{a denial of semantics}

spent your whole life searching for substance
maybe why you shoot your load on a daily basis

{all those elements surrounding absolute zero}

first they'll try to annihilate you and when they see that this task
is not so simple go to idolizing you, and when you prove to be repulsed
and disgusted by such base, vulgar (self-loathing) instincts (not wanting a
part of any one of them) go back to the one which proves to be a little less difficult

those who sit in silence while malicious and parasitic rumors
and gossip are spread are just as guilty and criminal as those
cowards who need to feed and function and thrive off this dynamic

the pure glee and essence of a child or adolescent
as there still has not as of yet been anything discovered
or full explanation on a physiological or psychological level
to attribute such an empirical or spiritual phenomena of spirit

{a freudian aphorism}

nightmares and dreams are all those feelings
on the edges and deepest core of the subconscious
which otherwise could not be expressed or comprehended
in waking reality often intermingled with those profound periods
and phases which appeared to hold the deepest meaning; take
for example as opposed to the functioning of your being in every
day reality when enlightened by the existence of fish and flora
and organisms beneath the sea; all that wild animal and plant
life enmeshed in the deepest recesses of the jungle and forests
the brilliant blazing stars which suddenly come out in the evening

{irregular verbs}

all those people who decide to commit suicide i always find
i have so much more respect for like suddenly decide some
time around 3:23 things just ain't going right or will never go
right and why not just blow their brains out and can't help

but to think about them with a deep and profound amount
of sympathy and affection as opposed to that population
of humans who will just never ever return phone calls

{folklore}

i always hated that expression–"don't put all your eggs in one basket"
if they only knew all your past damage would know all the reasons
you had to and wouldn't be making such declarative statements

{quotients}

1. getting 6th grade classroom photos back is great
2. i call it the jack-o-lantern phase
3. where they all just sit on stage glowing
4. with proud and hopeful wraparound smiles
5. and a whole mess of magical teeth missing
6. in some miraculous imaginative phase of denial

{civ 101}

when you find out the king & queen
you used to worship were simply

symbolic who just knew how
to work the system better...

life & times of
the pennypincher

of the psychiatrist
count backwards

to work on your anger
and make yourself

feel better
5,4,3,2,1

blast off
session over

combination of
stingy & greedy

waiting for the moon
to stop bleeding

for the sun to go
cockle-doodle-do

to the rooster
in the morning

only the truly cool people
know to enter the alley

to the saloon
true blue blues

goddamn fucken
nosh-eat-ing!

tourettes taught
me everything...

Vegas Way Before It Was Called Vegas

definition: bad/boy...never knew why they'd call him this
as about as nice and kind and loyal with mad spirit and generous
as you could get; sometimes rebellious the most pure core of virtuous

never knew why they'd call him this as would give them the clothes
off his back and food off his plate and could already see written all
over their face their petty jealousy and plans for betrayal and hate

never knew why they'd call him this and forced to go it alone and make a name
for himself like moses roaming the moaning desert for 40 years misinterpreted
as all he could do was move forward and didn't have time to watch his back

like clint eastwood, butch cassidy
and the sundance kid, meira lansky
starving for leftover boneless spareribs

never knew why they'd call him this and saw him as suspicious
as it was them who were so much more insular and ignorant and simply
seemed scared of themselves while appeared far more aggressive and ambitious

never knew why they'd call him this and could never ever begin
to know what it meant to be mislabeled and misjudged
and how wisdom is simply the self-image of what

it means to feel so alone as well as the remainder
of all these symptoms and patterns and
misperceptions by the status-quo

never knew why they'd call him this
and how ironically the true criminals
were them mind body spirit and soul

never knew why they'd call him this
as so much more experienced and courageous
and never knew them once to have taken a risk

never knew why they'd call him this
and thought maybe instead should
just take it as a compliment...

Word Problems

Those girls from elementary
        became an instant distraction
                to your sports & studies
    and suddenly sprang up
            like strange perennials
                  out of the fertile fields
those tomboys of the licorice woods
        who presented as so much more
                of a challenge & intriguing
    who might sentimentally complete
            your fragile & tragic self-destructive identity
                    with absolutely no rhyme or reason
and guess
    that was the hole
           illusory maddening point of it...

Zenith

i remember i used to go running home after school
everyday to watch the exact same version of 'peter
and the wolf' on channel 13 (used to be on one of
those *zenith* tv's where you'd actually have to get up
out of your chair to turn the dial or switch the channel)
and be all these strange young adults dressed up in
leotards i guess representing some sort of symbolic
hunter or animal prancing all around with extra zest
and gusto, and way too much imagination (people i
swear i'd even get embarrassed for) with always that
very histrionic and melodramatic symphony constantly
repeating bringing about a certain amount of melancholy
and used to think and sincerely believe that something
new might happen, but of course, never did, and
knew it was a parable for something yet never really
knew what for, where i think actually may have even
made me situationally depressed, which ironically felt
very much like the grand metaphor for all life and existence.

Silverware

reflecting
looking back
to the hangouts
of my youth right
around dusk it
always seemed
a certain shade
of purple when
i was always
flooded with
emotions
deserted
and lost
confused
conflicted
between
guilt and love
not sure what
to make of it
constantly
feeling pressure
like i was doing
something wrong
almost like those
racing thoughts
creeping home
through delicate
developing shadows
from the shopping mall
through the suburban
brush of strangers
backyards with
a rubber cement
moon beginning
to form which
only made me
feel so much
more alone
somehow
making it home
to sense and scents
of your mom's supper
(even silverware being
a strange trigger) which

helped me to instantly
forget but also remember
when i grew up my girl
friends and even wife
would say i play this
constant push and pull
game or crazy borderline
girl i might have loved said
she loved me because she
knew there was always some
part of me where she couldn't
get close or that i was this
interesting cross because
i was a classic guy (guess
the primal kind) but also
another side which was
very sensitive never really
thought too much about it
but when she brought it up
think i might have liked this
still finding myself overwhelmed
by dusk or what they like to refer
to as the bewitching hour or for that
matter that they even cared enough…

The Local Express

I don't know if it's just me...
but frequently I've had more respect
for the promiscuous ladies on the train
(often I'd have more respect for them
because they would come on to me
& you could tell they were just lonely
girls in a lonely world & in the moment
just trying to escape a lonesome reality)
rubbing up against me literally in the early
morning knowing exactly what they were doing
me in my construction boots & 5 o'clock shadow
& flannel & often they'd be like executive secretaries
or even lawyers (one of those lost souls in human
resources or medical records) in a world where no one
seemed to really care or give a damn, just straight-up
survival on a daily basis where pharmacies would get
robbed, stocks drop & the elevator repairmen just show
up at dusk so what were the options & was the choice
really so bad to mutually get turned on while rubbing
erogenous zones back & forth in the out-of-control
very controlled beat & rhythm which became only
that much more intimate because of course were
strangers & could feel every shape & contour in
slow-motion & in that moment really did feel like
nothing else existed (& in truth nothing did) aroused
& turned on in this bumpa da bumpa ridiculous &
repetitive existence & lived in the moment feeling
chosen like some 15 minute of fame movie star or
stud gigolo leading man when used to being just
some sad pathetic voyeur in the crowd & going
out of your way to remember this experience &
maybe even them for the remainder of the day.

The Old Country

My grandmother who used to live
in one of those pretty big sunken
living room apartments in Jamaica
Queens with a view of the yards
and all of those smashed-up
deserted trains used to read
the obituaries religiously
on a daily basis and the butt
of jokes in our family (me
having a pretty keen sense
of humor never quite got it
and ironically they felt just
as guilty for scapegoating
having nothing else better
to speak about) and looking
back at that need for isolating
and heartfelt routines and rituals
with those gorgeous exotic sunsets
that only pollution can naturally make
fading behind those beat-up old trains
when you live alone and nostalgia
and the imagination takes over
can you really at all blame her?

Blues Is Brooding 1:23 In The Afternoon
Truly Having Nowhere To Go On 145th
& Amsterdam In The Sweltering Summer

I think my greatest times
was just after I got engaged
and became a social worker
reading Nietzsche in the autumn
parks of Harlem outside of high
rise projects not sure if those
leaves were falling from
sycamores or the heavens
any which way felt
like confetti or some
form of redemption
knowing I wouldn't
be mugged or shot
(always hated that
stereotype bullshit
& gossip more
often coming
from those
who hadn't
seen a thing
in their lives)
while was just
as down & out
minding my own
business so all was
(i)relevant or relative
and taken me so many
long suffering solitary
years of seclusion &
searching to become
a fatalist or someone
of slight wisdom
meeting up with
classy older black
women in the spare
bones of their apartments
providing them their S.I. checks
who were kind & compassionate
& grateful for the little they had
and loved listening to every last…

Talk Therapy

The hoity-toity even during periods of crisis and suffering
will try to maintain and retain that baseline of hoity-toity
hoity-toity, hoity-toity, hoity-toity, hoity-toity (sounds like
some Yiddish version of the tidy bowl man) as for me when
ever I'm feeling really low or down in the dumps will stick
my head deep down the staticy mouth of the clown (to
my roots and origins) in order to order a cheeseburger
and onions and feel I can relate or make a real connection
with society and culture maybe even put in a couple good
words and flirting with the cute girl at the window and take
off a new man feeling like maybe just maybe I might belong.

This Is A Wreck/ording

Right before the apocalypse all you hear over the scratchy speaker
is–"Thank you for your patience" always ironically coming down
to this and turns out to be that infamous recording of "thank you
for your patience" with skulls bones bloody limbs scattered in
every which direction pure trauma and carnage of "thank you
for your patience" while one of the candidates is out in Vegas
trying to get the Hispanic vote and ordering her enchilada
in Spanish and the other one down in The Deep South
looking like Frankenstein in a pair of *Levis* boogying
in an all-black Methodist church while this real-life
billionaire bigot will be seen eating black-eye peas
and fried chicken and cornbread and grits (for
the primaries in Iowa of course it's a pork chop
on a stick trying to convince all those out of work
and on unemployment that they're one of them)
and due to the nature of recent affairs of inclement
weather and propaganda and the apocalypse also get
swept up and blown to pieces with that collective big
brother repetitive recording of "Thank you for your patience."

Joseph D. Reich

A Different Sort Of Pillow Talk

He picks up the three girls
hitching beneath the mountain
in their field hockey uniforms.
they survey him and look him up and down
and then like they usually do with that natural
rapport just among themselves jump right in.
he likes to hear them chatter because knows
even if he tried couldn't keep up with them
as still so impressed and in awe of these rare creatures
who keep this animated conversation (its pace and cadence)
going throughout the journey as if he does not even exist
and perversely savors it and learns that much more.
when they finally reach their destination at the end
of some long-lost nondescript suburban dead end
the three in the back let out a couple more guffaws
and leap out while the one in front in one fell swoop
which feels like some slow-motion maneuver leans
over cocks her head and plants an open-mouthed kiss
right on his lips. not knowing what hit him she slips
out as well with a giggle and sprints away oblivious
with that field hockey stick lifted in the air and
suddenly out of nowhere unbeknownst to him he
just lowers his head and starts to weep out-of-control
while decides this time to take the scenic route home.

The Shape & Form Of Mist & Fog

in the morning while sitting on the head
                i stare out my stormy window
looking at the sulking sunflowers
                against the barn
& after a night of night
                mares
reminds me that i am
        here & no longer there
reminds me of those
          dope addicts
i used to know
            nodding-out
on the corner
        in san francisco
                at dusk
& strangely enough provides
a sense of belonging
perspective & trust.

The Origins Of Billy The Kid

One can really see when the mountains start to take shape
& form with all its folds & contours in the change
of seasons; when the spirits slowly start to stir

up in the chilly brisk air & the rivers & water
falls become more swollen, romantic, raging
radiant, all the different hybrids of trees

like bushels of multi-colored, fiery hay,
crimson, scarlet, yellow-blaze, pumpkin
the luscious crumbs of your imagination

billy the kid wiping his tired brow
with his bandana hanging in there
having been framed once again…

A Portrait –for William Carlos Williams

The kids sled down the steep hill of the neighborhood radio
station at dusk with just that blinking red antenna above and
Pearl Jam crooning–"she can't find a better man." The stars
twinkle that much clearer and brighter in the brilliant winter
night way above the mountain. It is important to note as well
that there is a tall skinny red-haired girl who just stands silently
contented on the corner across from that covered bridge which
crosses the frothing river. She gives the impression of being
nowhere but feels very much like somewhere and looks like
a subtle stunning and reflective portrait, and could spend the
rest of your life staring at her even if your life depended on it.

Joseph D. Reich

Bridesmaid (on suicide watch)

America Online reminds us
a funnel was discovered
on Mars; Jeeze-Louise
wonder if that was
Missy Levine from
Suny-Binghamton
who used to carry
that beer funnel
around with her
over the week
end and drink
all the boys
under the
table?

Those Creaky Steps Of Growth & Development

1. i started off a fool...
(acting-out just to get approval)

2. became a fragile king...
(with first love gorgeous girl
from germany where's she? where am i?)

3. then a fool once more...
(playing dumb for purposes of pure survival)

4. thus have seen it all...
(can't get a thing over on me)

5. combination of harpo & leo gorcey...
(pu-pu platter lit on fire by the delivery boy)

6. put a gun to my head...
(and out shoots a bouquet of flowers)

Joseph D. Reich

Social Work: don't be a stranger

1. all's i remember was living
in that motel down in texas

2. right next to these llamas
behind some broken electric fence

3. and had me hospitalized 'cuz sick of being bullied by them
by those kids and eventually told them i was gonna kill them

4. i used to walk home from the mall
a couple miles in 100 degree weather

5, just recently in my late-thirties gave me the diagnosis of asperger's
'cuz my parents were always too busy and left me at home watching tv

6. i remember they used to feed me cups
of red wine to get me to sleep in my crib at night

7. my dad took off and left
my mom driving the truck

8. she passed-on and left me with my uncle
up in vermont who used to steal my bucks...

9. ...now lives with a kinder old man a retired veteran
who makes airplanes all day long down in his basement

10. and upon meeting him explained to me
how he thought obama was worse than hitler

11. but still am able to do home visits at least twice a week
and get him out into the community most specifically

12. to walmart where he is able to spend his stip-
end however he wants and goes up and down

13. each and every aisle like a literal fine-tooth comb
shuffling sideways checking out very precisely

14. every flavor of ice cream such as pumpkin
(his celebration of the seasons) he keeps down

15. in the extra freezer in the basement and having the ability
to have his own free will and volition to him is like heaven...

Progress Notes

These days i feel a lot like those
            girls i used to work with
                      out at those group homes
     in newport, rhode island
           who were removed from their homes
                     'as deemed to be a threat to them
selves or others'
    & would cut them
               selves
in the effort
      to try &
           feel again
                              & it was all so damn surreal
                  cuz the great big window in the living room
             had a view of the navy yard & the river & could see
                       ships stealing away on the horizon
   as was assigned to do
            car therapy with them
                  to get them
                        out of their mileau environment
                                 & in a state of flux
     while being a native new yorker
couldn't help to control myself from
cussing at rush hour yet ironically
think they really appreciated this
& were able to relate to me
& make a connection
       drifting past the casinos
to the stray dogs on shore
       & now looking back to those days
                 of being a social worker
                          not sure who i am more?
     those lieutenants in the navy?
          myself cussing at rush hour?
                  those stray dogs?
                or those poor girls
                      cutting themselves
       in the attempt to try
& feel again?

Axe Body Spray

Poor boys i used to see
in those schools in those
depressed new england
towns where their mothers
all turned to drugs and now
living with their grandmothers
and seeing all those commercials
for *axe body spray* where when
you sprayed it on you instantly
got all the girls and the pattern
i discovered the ones who wore
the most the less they got and
stuck in the adjustment counselor's
office reeking of really cheap cologne
playing that game operation and hearts.

The Graveyard

I think i want to get
one of those jobs
where you like
deliver people's
internal organs
back & forth
between hospitals
as might just give
my life a little
purpose
& meaning
but knowing
my luck & hx
will probably
end up towing
my sorry ass
back & forth
with people's
melting hearts
& souls
& kidneys
& spleens.

A Found Poem: America for $11.25 an hour

Part 1:

Production Team Member - 2nd shift
$11.25 an hour
VT Peanut Butter is growing and looking for production team
members on 2nd shift. If you feel you meet the requirements
of this position, please send in your resume for review.

Duties/Responsibilities;

Operate Manufacturing equipment as required
(Grinders, Blenders, Fillers, Labelers)
Perform end of shift cleaning tasks
Perform shift standard work tasks
Maintain food safety protocol during the manufacturing process
Completes all quality related inspection requirements
Complete necessary paperwork and documentation to ensure quality
conformance and product control
Actively participates in process improvement activities
Adheres to all Safety guidelines and procedures
Other assignments as required

Skill and Experience Requirements:

High School Degree required
Prior Manufacturing experience required
Food Safety experience preferred
Strong communication skills required
Team player who contributes to creating a safe and productive work environment
Ability to cross train and learn new tasks within the manufacturing process
Prior process improvement experience preferred
Reliable
Dependable
Maintain a clean an organized work area
Follow all policies and procedures
Escalate any issues through the leadership team for resolution
Ability to work Over time if needed

Part 2:

As an Assembler you will be responsible for producing
a quality product in an efficient manner, per instruction;

and in accordance with company policies and procedures.
Apply Now if you meet the qualifications listed below!

Responsibilities for this Assembler job include:

• Arrive on time. Clock in and out appropriately, for work finished; use comments appropriately to identify problem areas. Notify a manager of any error in clocking in or out or quantities so that it may be corrected.
• Read and follow work instructions. Sign all work as instructed.
• Assemble Parts on an Assembly Line. Must be able to work a minimum of half the scheduled day on team assembly lines and meet minimum time requirements accurately and consistently in repetitive environment.
• Rotate through all Assembly areas as assigned.
• Follow visual inventory replenishment rules at every station, including the proper care of empty boxes.
• Perform visual inspection of assembly parts.
• Ask a Trainer, Line Lead, Dept. Lead or Quality Manager when there is a question of quality. Quarantine nonconforming parts through reject processing system. Fix own rejects as they appear on your schedule.
• Complete 5S (Sort, Set in Order, Shine, Standardize, Sustain) before leaving any work station. Clean: process rejected parts, put tools in allocated areas, pick up any trash or loose parts and fasteners from floor and station surface. Sweep immediate area.
• Make ergonomic adjustments to tools, balancers and lift tables at stations where available. Use proper body mechanics.
• Follow safety rules including proper use of PPE (Personal Protective Equipment) and report safety concerns and injuries to the Floor Supervisor, Dept. Manager, Manager, and/or Human Resources.
• Report tooling issues to Floor Supervisor or Dept. Manager.
• Maintain level of productivity and quality in accord with business needs and expectations set by management.
Physical Requirements

• Able to lift and carry up to 50 lbs. frequently.
• Able to push/pull carts with up to 50 lbs. frequently.
• Able to stand on concrete floors for extended period of time.
• Able to walk frequently in the course of job duties.
• Able to twist up to 45 degrees on a frequent basis.
• Able to climb stairs to reach to the production floor.
• Able to crouch, kneel and reach on a frequent basis.
• Able to consistently grip tools required for the job duties up to 80 lbs. of pressure.
• Able to pinch product used in assembly with 20 lbs. of pressure on a frequent basis.
• Able to participate in daily mandatory stretch break.

First and second shift positions, Monday – Friday, 1:30PM - 10:30PM.
Pay for this position will be $11.25/per hour.

Adecco provides one of the most comprehensive benefits packages
in the industry to contract workers.

Part 3:

On the most vague ("opaque") of days
which feels like plague, employee
discovered gray and unwilling...

Certain Such Elements

***

Doesn't all life
sometimes seem
like a strange inside
job we are all whole
heartedly unaware of?

***

Time to throw butterfly kisses to the wind
when the tombstones shimmer best at dusk
and all the single girls shuffle home from work
melancholic, humble, thoughtful, and to die for

girls so radiant you wouldn't even
want to bring home to your mother

***

"Phoooey! Phony baloney!"
how come people don't use
words & phrases like that
anymore as looking back
to my childhood seemed
to say it all while sliding
down that huge baking-
hot metallic slide burning
my backside in my cut-
off corduroys in the back
of the y landing as always
safe & secure in that eternal
mass of sand & later at dusk
'cuz didn't do my homework
when my conscious & guilt
kicked in (what a maddening
& complex feeling) brooding
about life & death & mortality

***

Ran into my kid in the hall
as randomly told me he had
too much time so decided
to draw a goblin told him
that made perfect sense
and he seemed satisfied
and we both parted our
own separate ways…

heard him singing
the rest of the day

***

It's funny boys still hate
to get their hair combed
and put up a big fuss
and struggle and tussle
with their mom, doesn't
change much when you
get married and older
and she's picking
up your crumbs

***

Baby i still love you just as much
as when i brought you home to
meet my mother during thanks
giving in the berkshires and
made out in the bathroom
and could feel every draft
and element of winter through
the keyhole with the woodpile
lit under the stars and still got
that exact same zen-buddha
madman spirit swinging
ponytail from the bronx

***

Tonight driving her a little crazy
i went into a natural refrain of–
"who is that little girl i married?"
she said she was gonna' punch
me in the face. she's from
that place where they take
things quite literally–

"sunrise, sunset
sunrise, sunset…"

***

I want to see her
dance out of her
flowery shower
jump into her
purple sun
dress and
ask who
is that
i love it
"cobra
on my left
leopard
on my right"
(she was
born in 77)
we should
have walked
down the aisle
to "cops in cars
the topless bars"
7 & 7's on the
slow local
baby all
the way
to heaven
o yeah
james
douglas
morrison

***

-Hey look it's a full moon
-It's not a full moon...
-Yeah it is look out the window
-It's a harvest moon
-How do you know?
-The radio...

***

Why do i always seem to get advice from people
who i couldn't care less to get it from (nor do they
have the insight or judgment or perception or real life
experience) but in periods of crisis when i'm needy
and desperate there is never ever anyone around

***

This morning going back & forth with my wife
about the simple idea & notion of honesty
simply broke it down to would make our
lives proportionately so much easier
& wouldn't have to waste all this time
& wouldn't have to go back & forth
with these constant debates & semantics
& power-struggles & would cut down
on so much time & trust me won't lose
any respect for her or any of that female
mystery or je ne sais quoi & didn't quite
exactly work & went off on more examples
& checks & balances & all i could really do
at that point right there in the moment in the
kitchen over our morning coffee was start singing
billy joel's classic off that brilliant album the stranger
(i mean what else can a dude do?) 'i can always find
someone who say they sympathize...but i don't need
some pretty face to tell me pretty lies...' as she stormed
off very seriously & passionately & responded–"try that with
someone new" and went "someone new? i don't understand
that?" as deep-down inside think was kind of the whole point

***

One needs multiple-personality disorder
(in order) to survive marriage

almost all forms of marriage
is a form of embalming...

Fall Foliage (or at the bottom of a box of crackerjacks)

After waiting for like forever for the doctor to show up
when he finally did and asked me who i was i said
i wasn't and had a sex change. i told him i was
sorry and acting-out and was just such a long
wait, then went on with erica in the corner
providing him my medical hx–'doctor
i don't feel comfortable, she threatens
to stab me every night but makes me
feel closer' even offered him to finally
put me to sleep and gave him full
consent and approval and could
use a horse tranquilizer like when
keith moon passed-out poignantly
over his drum set in the middle
point being doctors please stop
making your patients wait more
than a half hour; anyway think
he appreciated it and had a grin
the whole time while at the end
of his career, a much older guy.
i told erica when we drove home
through the corn he looked like
the speaker of the house and for
some reason she cracked-up; was
really referring i think to that schmuck
mitch mcconnell and then after all that
waiting and losing your patience they tell
you you have elevated blood pressure; what?
you think? at least i got a referral for a rheumatoid
specialist at *dartmouth-hitchcock*. when we got home
our fine son hanging out with that cool kid who was in
the traveling circus and parents acrobats from slovakia
told us with pride how he very responsibly made
himself a microwave dinner and hydrated…

How To Survive & Cope The Overthrow Of A Government
At One Of Those All-Inclusive Resorts

Was thinking of escaping it all and especially when the wife
and I have a little money and time to kill and kid off from school.
Go on Expedia and fly away from Burlington International Airport
to places like Cozumel or somewhere in Central America but they
must have rooms right on the beach with palm trees and a view
of the sea, and found this one where everything seemed to be
honky-dory, blue and glistening, yet think might have seen on
one of the TV's I think in the junior suite where the government
was being overthrown, but really didn't give a damn just as
long as it's glistening and blue and has a view of the sea

Keep on reading glossy magazines feeling no pain with a buzz
from a banana daiquiri and a smile they just can't steal from me.

Off Season

sometimes when i have nightmares
i coil myself on the couch naked
in the fetal position in front of
the television in front of
the wind in front of
the weather in front of
the tropical depression
whose gyroscopic warnings
look like some colorful gob
stopper spinning slowly back
wards on its back break dancing
(like a dreidal) on its axis accident
ally don't care if there's some strange
spirit out there all by its lonesome
carrying some lantern in the woods
weeping if they find me in bloodred
sheets from an ap:parent suicide
may that bloodred rose still be
balanced in my overbite with
a coy smile looking forward to
the afterlife should have turned
towards opium (stead of the slums)
ie. love potion the scholars speak
so highly of slow-motion and
on-the-run but got stoned in
the sunflowers with all the bums
all alone by the barn with the white
chickens and william carlos williams
should have had a killer instinct but
never had one who am i kidding
always had one should have had
another kid always was a kidder
smoking my cigar like harpo
(jesus h.) playing harp on his
harmonica cracking riddles
at my own expense unable
to keep myself out of harms
way (hell that's all overrated)
to an awe dense didn't care
less if were there or not (as deep
down inside knew was wanted
unwanted dead or alive) knew
myself too well to know a cigar
sum times is just a cigar ease a

cigar is a cigar is gertrude stein
mocking (her mom wishing to be
her hero dad) shmoking a sea gal
trying desperately to just be come
infamous not ambitious and influence
ernest hemingway and alice b. tolklas
to know if you really look deep enough
into the soul all of your dreams lie at
the core of your fears of your amoeba
nucleus symbolic prodromal night mares
(don't need a freud ian to tell to steal you that)
just pals you lost some where? down the line
who now have become strangers and to die for
doe-eyed girls with powdery alabaster complex
shuns suddenly worship you by the out-of-order
hellevaders innocently looking for a savior both
desperately trying to find your way back
home to the original traumatic trigger.

A Life Lesson For One Of Those Life Lessons

i don't trust humanists like i don't
trust kiss asses, martyrs, and good deed doers
matter of fact who'd even want to be called a humanist
or probably, most likely, something they just invent
or call themselves or refer to themselves as
with just way too much time on their hands
and sounds like someone who can afford
it or just has all the right connections
looks like they all look and dress the same way
but got that expression on their face like they
haven't had intimacy or good sex in ages
what would you even say or ask a humanist
and thinking about it just makes me nauseous
or how would you hang out and what would you
do with a humanist as just puts way too much
pressure or expectations, and of that simply
makes me naturally, nihilistically suspicious
how you seem to always owe them put in a position
where you constantly feel guilty and have to ask
for their permission or forgiveness but in truth
and reality when it comes down to the nitty-
gritty are the ones so much more driven
and phony, shiesty and self-righteous
consistently playing mind games
full of see-through contradictions
and hypocrisies, self-interested
and opportunistic, so guess
when it comes down to it
prefer to stay away from
the humanists as just not
a big fan of them or don't
think too highly and can see
right through the high and mighty.

For Wittgenstein, H. Caufield, And Mark Twain

Act I

I always liked people so much more
before they made names for themselves
they just always seemed so much more
down-to-earth and humble and felt like
i knew them so much better and after be
came a bunch of aloof assholes composed
of those traits and characteristics of what
it meant to make a name for yourself while
after they made names for themselves act
or think that you really care so much about
the fact that they appear to have made names
for themselves as their whole existence revolves
around their reputations (or like personal pathetic
self-righteous resumes) or all about what people
think about them or breaking it down literally
succinctly to 'making names for themselves'

Act II

If they *really* make names for themselves
they always appear to be throwing brunches
or charity luncheons or award-giving functions
of actual plaques and awards at country clubs
or catering halls ironically given by the exact
same people and the same people are always
giving out trophies to the same people and always
run into these herds and parties of same people
and only see these same people at same people
gatherings of pure nepotism and who you know
and the who you knows surrounded by who you
knows surrounded by more who you knows or i
guess that special breed or class and culture of people
who made names for themselves until you take off not
feeling too much at all or even worse off feeling nothing at all

Joseph D. Reich

Act III

The most important act or part or thing of all is how
often you show up to funerals or can afford to show
up to weddings or afford to show up to weddings
and funerals and then can develop a reputation
based purely on this effort and function on the
accumulation and amount of times of showing
up to weddings and funerals or doing your life
long tour of showing up to weddings and funerals
and then become something of the personified life
of the party or death of the dying or getting back
to your origins in trying so hard to earn a reputation
in making a name for yourself and have become some
name for yourself until it's your turn for your time to go.

For Louis-Ferdinand Celine

One would think with all the phony and pathetic hypocrisies
and contradictions of human nature, there'd be so many more
hostage situations on a humanistic and existential level; gagging
and blindfolding the immediate and extended family finally able
to explain yourself, and all the challenges and obstacles you had
to overcome and endure all by your lonesome, of which these
conformists and followers would have absolutely no idea or
comprehend with all their distorted thought patterns, aggressive
and filthy vulgar intentions, and false accusations, which they
are ironically so much more guilty of, then after a little while
when nausea sets in you realize you just want to get rid of them
as soon as you can; this room full of self-righteous, sleazy, higher
than holy buffoons, who you never ever even really wanted there
in the first place, while can hear them muttering under their breath
with a whole new set of ridiculous delusions and disconnects and
gossip and rumors all done at their own convenience, which in no way,
shape, or form comes by coincidence; how in looking back to your days
of education, all of those who acted so driven and virtuous really weren't
and it was the ones who couldn't keep themselves out of trouble (being wise
asses, acting-out, and sarcastic without a mean bone in their body) how the
regulars in detention hall who may very well have been the true-blue angels.

The Difference Of Denouements

My favorite part of Broadway always
right before the actors got up on stage
wondering the exact life stories of each
one of the members rustling in the pit of
the orchestra in the pit of my stomach
and much later on after I had earned
it passed-out in the back seat of
the car zooming up that dark
silhouetted highway away
from the madness of
the melodrama of
reality with all
those vehicles
stripped-down
and all the girls
you were gonna
score with this
time saying
just the right
thing taking
them away
to a lifetime
of safety
& security.

Life On The Planet…

Father just shows up to the head of the table
with that noose still naturally dangling around
his neck but all the kids have pretty much gotten used
to it as kids just being kids and being natural acrobats
and conversationalists and resilient ask without even
noticing and accepting and simply a part of things
'please pass the mash potatoes, pass the peas!
please pass the gravy' while he also ritualistically
and religiously shows up every evening creeping
up those basement steps from the garage with it
already tried on for size when he kisses his wife
and when he does the bills and falls fast asleep
in front of the sports and weather at night…

He earns a pretty good income but still some-
how can't help but feeling bit dead to the world.

Earth: a short film or play in the vein of the theater of the absurd

We just see this very good looking clean-cut young man
with a five o'clock shadow (brooding dark and handsome)
a tight t-shirt on framing his strong muscular body and jeans
(perhaps to be played by Joaquin Phoenix or what's his name
from *Buffalo 66*) sitting at the corner of a picnic table pushed
up against some bone-white wall in a dim courtyard playing
the role of a therapist. At the other corner of the picnic table
sitting directly diagonally across with his silhouetted back
and shoulders turned from the camera is the patient. We
discover through the lens of the camera that this a very
urban and spare and sparse shadowy courtyard probably
somewhere in The Bronx and can faintly see shots of the
faraway river for atmosphere and perhaps every so often
the distant sound of stray foghorns. All during the film
we just hear the thoughts of the therapist who is actually
also the mind of the patient yet somehow as well narrated
by this older man who we never see at all though the screen
window of a ground floor apartment which looks out to this
very spare scene and who we find out too is also coming from
his point-of-view and true in fact deep down inside the selfsame
patient making such ironic but very matter-of-fact existential solemn
statements like 'I've spent my whole life moving from place to place
to find peace and still can't find it and here I got this guy who is some
psychiatrist and breaks every rule in the book with his drinking problem
of fine cheap red wines and confidentiality' as we see this simple and spare
silhouetted scene frame by frame day in and day out throughout the movie
but turns out there's actually something quite self-soothing and cathartic
and healing about it. We see the life and the daily activities of this therapist
in a very regimented ascetic way supermarket shopping just picking up
and choosing things like fresh turnips and squash and parsnips for his
supper of roasted vegetables; the other shoppers from the neighborhood
know exactly who he is and what he does for a living and is well-liked
and a nice guy and well-respected because he keeps to himself and is
just as lonely and solitary and isolated and damaged as that is his back-
ground and heart and soul speaking, while the camera pans in and out
frame by frame day in and day out mostly to the silent solitary silhouetted
figure of this very handsome clean-cut young man with a five o'clock shadow
in that muscular t-shirt sitting in the corner at that picnic table against the bone-
white wall in that spare and sparse shadowy courtyard with a new patient everyday
and his back to the camera with a distant view almost as if through some alley or
aperture of that opaque river with stray foghorns coming through every so often.

Numb: a short film called "human resources"

i think a wonderfully macabre black & white film noir...
would show this individual very methodical and masterful
on a day by day even minute by minute basis going through
the protocal and process and routine and ritual of his daily
activities while ironically has these very neat and organized
files perfectly concretely labeled kept on file for at least a
year, 2, 3... like how it might be set up in "human" resources
(of how they tell you how long they'll keep your resume on file)
and then mechanically driving his car very focused through the bones
of some bare black & white absurd monochromatic suburb somewhere
sometime after dusk and following that very infamous head of human
resources home to her lost and lonesome existence and shows him
slowly choking or suffocating her getting some sort of strange pleasure
or partial arousal or inspiration out of it while each new frame will
exhibit him performing the exact same act of following some other
very distinct nondescript individual back to their domicile and then
at the end of each one perhaps pulling his resume out of a folder
and either lighting in on fire turning to ashes or putting it through
some shredder having removed it from that very organized area
maybe even re-labeling the folder with a convenient anacronym
like "na" of not applicable or in his subconscious really meaning
no longer available as the camera pans onto and does a close-up
of his own personal label ironically entitled "human resources"
moving on to the next frame showing him sitting at a small
table all alone contented with his tv dinner and bottle of wine
in a dark room in front of some laugh track/news program
(maybe covering him) in the spilled-out glow of television.

A Sci-Fi Fable: somewhere between redtape blues & blackmail

the anatomical figure wakes up and the first thing he does
like some sort of trickster or "thinker" stretches his spine
and skull; puts all the folklore and people who wish him dead
(more succinctly anna freud's defense-mechanisms) to rest;
watches all the scrap metal trucks zoom and rumble (like
those with chemical dependency problems feening for their
next drug) because out here above the lake in the mountains
those with the most scrap metal, the more attention and more
they're afforded legend status for their self-absorbed identity.
the anatomical figure sluggishly crawls out of his delicate coma
which separates fantasy from reality (past forced and forced-on
situational phases and existences from domineering, overbearing
figures of authority of clinical narcissism and obsessive-compulsive
behavior, who just like to hear their same old repetitive cowboy
stories to keep their fragile and pathetic identities in order) and
now takes baby steps in front of that gigantic seasonal window
and with a smirk and wisdom reflecting way above them, way
past any sort of absurd cognitive distortion of false wishing and
faux ethical control which involves all that bullshit and brainwash
and betrayal; which allows them to function and higher up in
the hierarchal scrap metal chain of command anatomical man
shakes off all that flattery of rhetoric semantics and perverse
formal language made to keep him down and them above
the scrum and climb up the scrap metal heap of success to
their projected and targeted goal of what it means to be virtuous
in some ridiculous, affected, and authoritarian version of heaven.

A Strange Sociological Axiom

I got this sociological theory and hypotheses (or phenomenon...)
that one can get to get to really know the aesthetic and economics
and demographics of a specific neighborhood or town by traveling
around America and simply viewing the commercials for used-car
lots and used-car salesmen; their expressions and body language
and the herd-mentality or individualism of how they present
themselves, the nature of their schtick, and gimmicks and
punchlines and payoff to the joke and riddle; how serious
they take themselves (with that very symbolic eye contact
and handshake) the genders they include and how they are
used, and last but not least, the actual size of the lot, the cars
or trucks it stocks, how prices vary and fluctuate (how expensive
or economical) and the lay of the land and where they are located
heregoe, one can really get to know as well the nature and soul of
towns and neighborhoods of America, the personalities of its people,
their demographics, economics, school systems (its jokes and riddles
or how serious they take themselves) by watching used car commercials.

I also have a theory for the innocence of weather girls
and the jokes they tell (the clothes they wear) having something
to do with the true-blue quaintness and down-to-earth quality of the town...

Joseph D. Reich

The True (falsehoods) Of Advertising

Everything in america
always seems something
of this cookie-cutter
version of exceptionalism
with its tribunal of aloof
clueless over-confident
reality show judging
and if not some orgy
of binge ballroom dancing
or binge breaking down crying
or binge drinking or binge eating
or binge painkilling or binge dieting
or binge money making or binge corruption
or binge politics as usual or binge video
or binge tv watching or binge serial
killing or binge war or binge folklore
all you got leftover is 7 straight days
at so and so's for an all-out trough all
you can eat binge shrimp extravaganza.

Color Of Pool

1.

People with patriotic pride
    stake up their sturdy lanternmen
bald eagles & American flags
    somewhere around their driveway
like a bizarre overly-controlled manicured
    obsessive safe & secure manifest destiny

2.

What a weird way of being or rather not being
    think if Jesus returned he wouldn't even
know what to make of this or what to do
    like one of those psychotic labradoodles
made in a laboratory with an attitude sniffing
    all around then continuing on to the next stoop

3.

The paperboy doesn't even exist anymore
    but rather a divorcee with a drinking problem
not giving a damn thinking his wife's a whore
    running the streets right before dawn

4.

What to make of the waking state?
    Everything happens at dusk!
Has the subconscious ever said to its night
    mare what the hell are you doing in my dreams?

5.

Recently have thought to Google or GPS God
    surrounded by all these clones on their smartphones
& rich daughters of nepotism acting like know-it-alls
    gossip & rumors the language of the status-quo.

Triggers

Not too long ago I called one of those 1-800 numbers
for a step-in tub and some older woman from Minnesota
got on the phone and tried to set me up for an appointment
but apparently there were none in my area so told me she
would first send out a brochure and never got one then
of course every time around the supper hour she called
me up to ask if I got the brochure (while the nature and way
of our culture) just kept on calling around supper and took more
solace no longer caring anymore about that step-in tub but hearing
her self-soothing voice from Minnesota asking if I got the brochure.

Saints And Other Odd Things

I am convinced that my wife cleans so much
(and of that I am eternally grateful, trust me!)
is gonna just swallow me up with her vacuum
when I ain't looking while whining or staggering
down the hall and like that scene from "I Dream
of Jeannie" where you just see her eyes all stuffed
in that genie bottle drop me off at one of those
used vacuum shops in one of those depressed
New England towns when all the industries leave
town and turns to hookers and heroin and I'll just
live happily after on one of those dusty shelves
with a bird's eye view of that funeral parlor across
the road where those old men just hang out in their
inky suits with nowhere else to go and very politely
gossip every weekend with resentful wives from
the old country out at confession and that beautiful
red-haired milf next door stranded by her cheating
husband now responsibly, religiously with her
downtime going back and forth over her lawn
feeling very comfortable and that I belong
in this deserted abandoned town
that took off and hit the road
leaving just the steeples
and cobblestone and
a river that no one
ever got to know.

Down & Out In The Montreal Mall

All those ridiculous freaks and petty thieves and madmen
and disoriented old men asking the time (all providing
a certain kind of ambiance) and old lonesome aristocratic
women rummaging for gourmet food as if trying to retrieve
some sentimental romantic relic or artifact from their past
while at the same time wishing to be saved and rescued
and seductive blushing school girls making their moves
and try out their moves on clueless husbands in the aisles
and the disgusting pedophiles in their sunglasses and corduroy
coats and strange hats so no one will recognize them sidling up
like seething tutors who still live with their mothers and the big
black security guard keeps a close eye on you (you apparently
resembling something of a 'criminal' and so funny 'cause deep
down inside used to be a hustler, but no longer anymore and
can recognize them before they recognize you) and got nothing
better to do, unaware you are a social worker with a masters
but in a good mood and wait outside with my handsome kid;
for my wife picking up *poutine*, or french fries and gravy,
cheese melting, and now keep a close keen eye on him, who
seems pretty lonely and empty and pathetic and petty in his
repetitive ritual and routine; when you get back to the hotel
with a view of the bourgeoisie homes set back in the hills
you realize, mortality-wise, we just go through this life
trying not to be 'the very lonely man' and the freak and
the grotesque and 'the stranger' and it's just miserable
humanity who makes you feel these types of things
of down and out (and low self-esteem) trying pathetically
to underestimate you from their ignorant and insular, even
distorted and delusional worlds, while playing their 'ridiculous'
roles (and it's ironically these gross and vulgar, absurd arrogant
wannabes involved in their ridiculous role-playing, for example
like those satirical make-believe guards at the border, who ask
you and your wife such absurd and inane questions like what'ya
got back there and you tell them Halloween decorations and ask
why we haven't put them out yet; guess it's still late-September
and can't really explain it like some ludicrous exchange and power-
struggle with good ole Inspector Cluseau and give their best ballpark
try to try and make you always feel criminalized, while don't buy into
it and end up trying so much harder and get madder and more frustrated
when they see they can't rattle you, having done way too much of living
and in a sort of perverse, abusive way, thrive off it, while they ironically
are constantly crossing borders and boundaries and invading your privacy
and continue on with their useless, futile, make-believe lines, while seem
obsessed and fixated with constantly asking if we're carrying any tobacco

or firearms and think in the back of my mind if in fact really
carrying tobacco or firearms would I actually tell them? Or
maybe just pull an Andy Warhol and saying why don't you
just give me the question *and* the answer, getting all Joycian
like we don't have tobacco and firearms, but got toboggans
& Finnegan's but think that might just get under her skin
and get her all defensive and hostile again, and proceeds
with her 'fine line' of questioning asking why do we have
so much luggage for the weekend like guess two or three
gym bags and *Star Wars* backpacks filled up with our kid's
books of *Captain Underpants* is too much, and just like they
always do to get in their abuse start to pilfer through our luggage
and realize she's just an empty and vacant jealous little bitch
without a loved one, who projects to death, as they do this
every time with their abuse of power and harassment and
line of questioning, which never ever quite makes any logical
or linear sense) so getting back to the philosophical hypotheses
and existential statement that man just goes through this existence
trying not to become 'distant,' the very lonely man, freak-stranger
and realize (with all your living *and* dying) simply can't avoid it
and just fine by you and all you can really do is order in room
service where they strangely enough, not strange at all, got
conveniently grouped on the delivery menu certain stuff
as apparently these are the basic and fundamental things you
need to get by, like cigarettes and *Palmolive* and beer (which
sounds about right) and your wife and kid suddenly get back
in and kick in the door like a bunch of blissful and slapstick
cowboys at The OK Coral and realize how happy (no longer
with all that unnecessary nihilistic worrying) you are to see
them, your own version of what it means through cognitive
redirection to be satisfied and contented, which ain't all that
lousy, blue, manic, down and out, down-in-the-dumps emotion
staring out your window at those bourgeois homes set back in the
hills you can't really relate to after getting back from The Montreal Mall.

Feeling Lost & Lonely In The Very Schmaltzy And Fancy-Schmantzy
Tourist Streets Of Quebec City Turning To The Olympics On Your TV

i am convinced that i've never been convinced

i'd love to meet the last of a dying breed
never met the last of a dying breed
who are the last of a dying breed?
think i'm the last of a dying breed
thus consequently feel so lonely

looking out my 7th floor window in quebec city
to the brilliant st. lawrence river with freight liners
parked in port blinking all during the day and evening

the freaks who got nothing left to do but lean all day
with their backs up against the wall of the tobac shop
and pick up pints of brandy and vodka all hours of the day

the old evil soulless tourists who act like royalty try desperately
to stare you down in the lobby like you are some kind of criminal
or thief (are these those veterans candidates speak of so affectionately
who make america great? they strike me more so mean and malicious
ignorant and prejudiced; i'm still trying to find them) as you explain
to your son who the real criminals are; they're part of the tour group...

it appears as though the fake aristocrat and bourgeois
(not so sure of themselves) have to always sacrifice
or slaughter someone to get where they are while
those who really got it don't have to try so hard

it seems like they spend a whole lifetime
slaving or treating people like shit so they
can one day stroll around as mean old geezers
with snarling scowls and pastel sweaters around
their shoulders around manic/ured gardens of flowers

and you wonder how the hell they
can even have ceremonies for these
devils to get into heaven? ha! ha! ha!
is that the way they say it these days?

i have so much more affinity for the cleaning lady
as so kind and sweet and can tell just helping out
her family when she tells me of the couple states
she's been to with such a cute lovely french accent

pronounces it like "flor-i-da" and believe she's one
of those girls you'd throw it all away for even more
than a fictional audrey hepburn when she used
to play one of those meek peasant characters

you wonder how this hotel got all these stars
and wonder who the true critics are and wish
your life only came so easy with all this faux
furniture and lighting fixtures and pool which
i suppose is supposed to be the focal point and
imitative stone and plastic flora supposed to
be climbing up the wall leading down to some
dramatic staircase down to some very dramatic
classical piano surrounded by ropes where no
one (guess call it lounge singer) ever shows up

you sit in your floral chair in front of the great big window
looking over the whole holy harbor and somehow develop
a real connection for the olympics i guess from a canadian
perspective and always turn off to those individuals or those
groups of people who show such pride and honor for their
country then always feel the obvious cliched obsessive
compulsive need to whip out their flag which ironically
paradoxically always makes me feel so much more
alienated and less of sense of belonging and nausea

the two radiant glowing girls stand on the edge
of the world on the edge of the diving board
with perfect bodies to die for for synchronized
diving, intense, stunning, actually looking more
puerto rican than canadian up on top of the world
up above the beautiful bleak slums of rio and land it

and seem so proud and grateful just to land a bronze
as i feel just as moved and tearful while they literally
stand like heroic and noble graceful royalty (who really
seem sincerely loyal) and place a large gingerbread
cookie of a medallion over both their soaking bodies

i love the rugby players who go all out and sincerely
appear like they're sacrificing their lives for their country
with great big strong herculean bodies and blood and sweat
dripping down their temples with blood-stained gauze bandages
around their skulls after the battle and can't afford to do idiot buffoon
dances in the endzone or complain about every foul called against them
again i feel a real connection even finally at last something of a revelation

as i limp through my room with my swollen extremities wrapped up in
adhesive bandages arthritis 3 and an impinged hip while my wife and
kid return from the old city with dumplings and that's all need be said

you leave a day early and 2 computers are down at the border
backing everything up (schvitzing and throwing curses all around
your car) and even when you want to be liberated and on-the-run feel
cursed and just like one of those innocent victims they're always talking of.

Crime & Punishment (American-Style)

i've been feeling a bit down in the dumps and real tough on myself
recently secluding myself like raskolnikov accusing myself of a crime
i know i did not commit as perhaps all i need is a simple trip to the price
chopper and when one of those pretty young girls asks me if i need help
with my bags to the car instead of scoffing simply go yes (maybe even
a "yeah sure!" like curly from the stooges) to put it all in perspective
a proverbial walk down the aisle and go back and forth and make
a little small talk with some blushing dove who i'll think of when
i'm driving home beneath the blazing fall leaves to my domicile.

A Time Like That

i was in something of a funk having a hard time waking up
and the tv leftover from the night before suddenly came up
and it was *i dream of jeannie* with such a wonderfully weird
naive concept of this cartoon space capsule the exact same
shape of a genie bottle which happened to coincidentally be
lying right next to one and out steamed this magical plume
of some perfumed torso waiting to connect up with the skull
of barbara eden and then seductively shimmying and swooning
over towards a young clean-cut larry hagman in his late 60's
nasa astronaut uniform who at first looked shocked and startled
and then she suddenly kissed his cheek and his eyes just lit up
and came alive while this episode they were on some vacation
looking like somewhere on the technicolor hawaiian big island
and everyone was dressed up in these neat powder-blue suits
and yacht costumes and taking off in helicopters to take photos
with panoramic areal views of the mountains like your parents
slideshow presentations in the 1970's suburbs when it seemed
like there was something to actually live for and look forward
to in the future then that big blinding ball of sun came up over
the mountains and blinded me while with eyes closed i simply
romantically reflected to a clean-cut larry hagman and seductive
barbara eden way up on their breezy balmy terrace of their high-rise
schmaltzy hotel somewhere on the big island and somehow i guess felt better.

Amen:i:festo

I want to be
one of those
fucken eccentrics
who spends the rest
of my days & existence
in one of those beatup brilliant
bed & breakfasts with very few
guests set way back in the forest
of the mountains & all my room
has are waxy wide pine floors
brass headboard, a lantern, prison
batphone only used every so often
& a turn of the century trapdoor
in the floor whenever i want to do
one of my secret romantic escapes
into culture; one single frosty lattice
which looks out to the changing season
& fields full of bales of hay & sheep
& goat & ribbons of chimney smoke
& raw & radiant down-to-earth
to die for blonde-haired girls
tumbling downhill from the
foliage with wide smiles
who right on time with
their literal manifest
o in hand pay their rent
looking drained & spent
staying with their madmen.

The Tourism Industry

I remember being down in the south of france
and can speak a little of the language and saw
this school bus of girls suddenly pull up along
side the curb of a school bus of boys and both
dropped their dusty windows and spilled out
from them and started going at it with such
mad spirit and passion, giggling hysterical
challenging each others identities and egos
seductively howling going back and forth
with this comical rapport and it was all so
surreal like didn't even really have to know
the language and thought was not this image
and these emotions transcendent or was not
this 'the international language of love' and
felt like so much more or maybe so much
less and finished up my beer at some cafe
of bums feeling no pain feeling completely
free and anonymous and shuffled and
staggered under the influence following
some gorgeous milf mother with tight
jeans on who knew exactly what she
was doing and knew exactly what i was
doing which just made it so much more
intimate and intriguing into some perfume
shop, but then it suddenly hit and dawned
on me first what the hell was i doing in there
in the middle of some perfume shop in the
middle of the south of france and how could
i explain myself (how could anyone explain
themselves?) and what would i say to her
as just don't speak the language so well
and my needs had strangely become so
sudden and impulsive yet in the moment
felt maybe perhaps mutually interested
(how this imperative might be the panacea)
while took off back to my motel pleasantly
miserable in my mirthful state of melancholia

but felt pretty good dozing off with a buzz
in the late afternoon not knowing a living
breathing soul in the middle of nowhere.

Ralph Lauren

They seem to be celebrating the holidays even earlier
this year in america like about a month before halloween
as see some commercial on tv of that mythological god
in his bathing suit with that pretty emaciated goddess
to die for by his side taking that deep-sea dive in that
grotto probably somewhere around corsica or malta
in the deep-blue mediterannean with water trickling
down his 6-pack body and can pick up a bottle
at the counter at *macy's* while interestingly end
up experiencing the same sensation or range of
emotions of a certain type of guilt and salvation.

Art

    i now understand those water
                colors of those naked biblical gods
in loin cloths desperately reaching out
                    pleading for dear life to the heavens
i understand every stitch from those mammoth tapestries
        which include serf king & beast alike hanging from medieval times
i understand how those beautiful ballet stars
                        anatomical-wise naturally instinctively stretch out to the stars
i have experienced & understood betrayal on each and every level
                        from best friend to brother from sister to mother
& all i ever was trying to do
          was be diligent maintain keep on & mind my own business.
for every reason & these exact selfsame reasons
                  i avoid politics & human nature
(to a fault as much as humanly possible)
                    & after my handsome 6th grade son
adhd the distractible & not hyperactive kind i discover
                  having stuffed & folded his class photo
(main street middle school)
          in his backpack now all wrinkled
on the refrigerator
          inquire with great interest who all those kids
are we never met before
          & tells me all about this cute girl
they call "speedy"
          planted in the 1st row who is a tomboy
& can beat most of them without even trying.

Missing Puzzle To The Peace

late at night you roam the halls like an old security
guard at some hotel trying to become more secure...

you inspect pictures on your wall from your travels around the world...

van gogh's dying sunflower marinating in your sill...

muted tv with a tropical storm crawling up the coast...

what's her name in your microwave...

a bust of buddha...

crumbs from that homemade cake made
by your wife's best friend freshly-divorced...

postcards you used to frame from that second hand store
in providence, rhode island when you'd take out those
neglected, abused boys from the group home who were
far classier and cultured (inquisitive and insightful)
than any colleague who would give you that
wannabe cookie-cutter clinical nod in the hall...

experience i suppose teaches one to pick off all the bullshit and patterns
of liars and what they're not telling you is everything they are which i guess
in the long-run leads to streetwise to wisdom to becoming a very lonely man...

they say can't teach you intuition
as well as having a sixth sense
how the greatest breakthrough
the discovery and configuration
of figuring out the subconscious
but where do you go from there?

the connection of the senses to triggers and vice-versa...

cruise ships are parked in port and prefer the stray dogs...

Rush Hour (forecast…)

1 i was one of the creatures
who didn't make it in evolution
does that make me god damn it...

2 you spend the rest of your
existence carrying a monkey
on your back dragging an accordion

3 "anyone know a
place to get good
fried calamari?"

4 doing that quick turnaround
film-noir shoot 'em up pose
in the mirror of that fleabag

5 motel at the end of the strip
a derelict unable to afford the one
with the convention of cosmetologists

6 paranoid midgets with
briefcases stuffed with
pharmaceutical samples

7 but dream one day of being
found dead with a panoramic view
of that crude eiffel tower, remembered

8 as a good tipper by the arabic
bellboy and flamboyant concierge
and come to so-called terms with exiting

9 an absurd existence of wannabe wiggers
with their daddy's little souped-up engines
pretending to be all scary and intimidating

10 with cookie-cutter
pre-manufactured
suburban anger

11 a bowl of empty oyster shells
discovered outside
my keyhole

12 a deck of
unopened cards
and unopened rubber

13 a promised land
of shag carpet and
air-conditioning...

Domestic Violence Or Why White
Trash Still Live With Their Mothers

i was watching
one of these
idiot fucked
up formulaic
bullshit blow
up violent
commercials
for some
american
crap ola
movie
and then
all of a
sudden
like some
broken
mantra
i hear in
the back
ground
"the
critics
rave"
like
with
out
even
realizing
as some
how has
become
a staple
some
half
crazed
conscious
ness like
what the hell
would it take
anyway to be
come a critic
or be married
to a critic or

hang out with
a herd of critics
(would *bourson*
cheese and pigs
in a blanket be
a prerequisite?)
and why the heck
why they probably
invented yiddish
in the first place
or for that matter
make them rave
like what would
that entail anyway
looking like a room
full of freaken raving
critics and think
would prefer raving
lunatics and to just
make the critics quiet
or shut the fuck up
and whisper like
when people claim
they have some
personal relationship
with god like yeah right
like some drunken down
and out damsel with a drinking
problem slurring her words
at some bamboo bar down
in the panhandle of florida
or some other ridiculous
know-it-all blowhard
with some abuse of power
proclamation claiming
their personal relation
ship and got him on
speed dial as for me
don't know about all
those claims of personal
and seems so much more
professional and that of a
con like some telemarketer
trying to take advantage
and turn the tables on them
and fuck them up when they

try to call you up at dusk
after some long miserable
day in the social work field
and just want to take your
meal with your wife and
kid and start breathing
heavy and talking dirty
and interestingly ironically
just like those other ass
holes start to get startled
or hesitant and offended
and all of a sudden turn
very formal going
"sir, sir, uhh sir…"
and you excuse them.

Not For Nothing

Every Saturday evening
i like to simply watch
Wonder Woman as find
it to be so self-soothing
& actually quite revealing
speaking about the subject
of government conspiracies
& all this undercover
cryptic clandestine shit
with secret briefcases
& plot twists & robots
& I guess because
it's muted get
to see in parent
theses phrases
like (um-hmm)
(violent beeping)
(beeping resumes)
having to do with
those robots
which keeps
me all calm
& cool & true
Lynda Carter
really was
a fox
& a babe
& hot
& to die for
even way
before she
did her whole
slow-motion
fast-forward
spin from
reality to
the nether
world into
Wonder Woman
so much more
than any of our
present blonde-
haired bimbo
reality show

slut stars
with all
their
so-called
confidence
& know-it-all
dialogue as op
posed to back
then something
far more relatable
making a difference
like government
conspiracies
& secret brief
cases & robots
& Lynda Carter
with those very
handsome serious
square-jawed
straighttalking
undercover
detectives
out to save the world
during the cold war
when *YMCA* was
the theme song
& your eyes
all bloodshot
waiting for
your mom
to pick you
up for sin
a gog to
learn
your
half
torah
become
a man
& earn
a couple
a bucks.

Love, Exciting And New

Tonight after one of those real long draining days
I introduced my son to *The Love Boat*, one of those
really wonderful corny shows from the Early-Eighties
which used to just make things alright again and explained
to him how all these dramatic and comedy stars from other
sitcoms (as well as others you just didn't know where they
came from) would just show up to the ship each and every
weekend with issues and marital problems and try to find
ways to cope through some form of romance or hope and
told him about the whole crew; Julie the cruise director,
who in real life had a cocaine problem; Isaac the bartender
who did that cool quick brother move everyone was so fond
of; Gopher who did odd jobs; the captain, Meryl Steubing
with those very high white knee socks and the oversexed Doc
who tried to make it with all his female patients and passengers,
and they only seemed to stop in Puerto Vallarta for some bizarre
reason which we just accepted and the whole show was just them
trying to resolve all their very petty absurd grownup psychodramas,
and when they finally returned safe and sound into port and disem-
barked they were all magically resolved with great big smiles as if
living happily ever after, bid farewell by Julie the cruise director with
the coke problem, Gopher who did the odd jobs, the ship's captain
with those very high white knee socks (somehow Isaac seemed to
conveniently be left out) and Doc who tried to hit it with all the
female passengers; my kid seemed to really appreciate it and
it did, not by coincidence, seem to make things proportionately
better, while we mutually decided we might try start making it
a family tradition to watch The Love Boat at 8:00 every weekend.

Sophistication

I fell asleep in my easy chair
to the theme for *The Bob Newhart
Show* and it was one of those really
good dreams where I was making love
with past girlfriends but guess it wasn't
that good as some past jealous boyfriend
tried to slit my throat and suddenly one
of Bob Newhart's patient's showed up
on the windy sill of 1970's Chicago
and tried to talk myself down...

American Existentialism

I:bid It's funny but in bringing in some of my kid's clothing
he's grown out of to one of those thrift shops or secondhand
children's stores on the strip mall which have all become so
organized and formal in what they will accept or not due to
current standards and criteria of present day adolescent needs
and wants and trends, found the lady behind the counter was
so much nicer and kinder and compassionate in providing me
an in-depth and insightful explanation to why she could not take
them and even more objective and supportive and offered to walk
me out to my car with my bags of clothes to help me get them back
in as think just viewed me as one of those 'gentle giant' fathers who
didn't quite get it or was not up to date or out of touch, but naive and
caring and generous and making an effort as compared to I swear some
of these so-called scholarly presses who for the most part don't even get
back to you or when they do are so practically and pathetically rude (aloof
and arrogant, all-knowing and abusing power of such poor character and
moral fiber like some supposed grownup almost appearing as if trying
to get back at you for being picked on their whole youth, something
you had absolutely nothing to do with and was always so kind
and compassionate and never a part of any one of those absurd
and mean-spirited, hypocritical cliques, and now ironically have
become just as 'judgmental and alienating' with their ridiculous
and reactive behavior and proclamations) when maybe perhaps
you were submitting a life's work with true mad and unique,
sincere creativity, wisdom, and passion, but didn't present it
in the exact fashion or persnickety prerequisite format that
universities (or 'scholarly' presses) in America so rigidly
now require and adhere to and obsessed with and so
concrete (abstract and ambiguous are not sure what
they're getting at) as the directions or how they anally-
retentively want you to structure and set it up (the control
freaks that they are) become so 'absurdly' complicated or
more important and significant than the actual substance
while ironically don't have an original idea or thought
(or true experience in the 'real world') more so focused
and fixated on the way they annotate or footnote and
'present their paper' yet not so interestingly, ironically,
writing or researching about other people's philosophies
(or philosophers) or methodologies or realities with absolutely
nothing original of their own. Funny, please forgive me but find
my most perceptive and keen times were at those high school
keg parties in the deep dark cold warmth of autumn in some pal's
backyard when their parent's took off for the weekend just vibing
with friends and acquaintances and hilarious slapstick trial and error

efforts with the young girls you never got with, returning home
all by your lonesome brooding and reflecting through damp romantic
evenings of leaf piles and lamplight and pools of shadows to things
which may have appeared more 'normal and familiar' (while all those
silhouettes and the holy silence of the suburbs, strangely enough,
introspectively and thoughtfully, felt it just as much in that solitary
'distant' un/familiar journey) whereas in the destination, paradoxically,
never quite exactly with all the repetitive brainwash and manipulation
of an overbearing authority figure and hostility and explosions from
a jealous sibling all feeling actually more criminal, as compared to
the recent spontaneous magical rapport of what you just experienced
over the last couple of hours which felt transcendentally like a lifetime

I:bid We have a tendency to make it a tradition to complain
about our fate and the state of our existence in what we like
to refer to as 'the greatest nation' in the world and remember
when I was going to The Wurzweiler School of Social Work
in my second year of internship at The Kingsbridge Center
for Rehabilitation in The Bronx right around the reservoir
while a majority of the janitorial staff and maintenance
were men and some of the nicest people I have ever
met who used to be top-notch doctors and surgeons
in the recently disbanded Soviet Union and were
hard-working and diligent and never once thought
to complain about the nature of their existence, and
remember during lunch breaks used to love to sit back
and chat with them about certain Russian authors I was
fond of like Pushkin and Dostoevsky and Turgenev and
Anna Akmanotav and Zukovsky and Mayakovsky, and
were so impressed that I had read them and knew all about
them but if they only knew how much more I was impressed
by the strength of their character never once exhibiting self-pity
or defeatism having been wealthy doctors and now janitors getting
paid shit and in all truth and reality getting absolutely no validation or
respect when it came down to it by the obnoxious, all-knowing administration

I:bid Is it just me but with the holidays coming around the corner
does it not appear like they are just inundating us with non-
stop commercials showing gigantic glistening diamonds
no one can truly afford and show some poor sucker
dropping to his knees asking her to marry him and her
instantly nodding her head, tearfully, ecstatic, deferential
and now she's all his (which puts instant pressure on him)

as now become an instant possession and he of course
an instant slave to try and pay it off on some payment
plan and will step into that store in the mall to confirm
with a contract and ratify it and now love and romance
has taken on a whole different reality and turned into
something of a legally binding document and better not
get laid-off or be able to pay it off as all those future
dreams and plans of yours might just vanish in thin
air and perhaps even your future put in question
(while your heart and passion hasn't changed
and remains the same but your ability to dream
and remain sane) while you instantly imagine
the strange image of yourself getting tossed in
midair like some bundled-up newspaper back in
the day right into the mailbox which appears to be
your wish-fulfillment or fantasy of freedom while
at the same time safety-security and arrested stage
of development having a difficult time moving your
neck due to stress and arthritis and inclement weather

Soon they will roll out the Chevy's and Lexuses
give you the actual figures over your television...

I:bid These days the skylines look all too perfect and pretty and pristine
(like Lego kingdoms) and present under such headings like 'business
cities' (with those very pithy and ridiculous statistics like 'best place
to start a new life' or 'raise a family') while the citizens with their
convenient contraptions appear delusional in their destinations (and
know exactly what they are doing and where they are going). Used
to be something to be said about gritty and mystery and uncertainty

I:bid Haunted ship slips into haunted port
to the haunted lighthouse in front of
haunted forest as all is haunted and
the man who runs the lights and
foghorns nodding-out completely
oblivious making it all too clear
and obvious there is no sense
of fairness while all is futile
and nothing at all matters

I:bid When the first malls sprouted and got laid-out
thought they'd be the answer to all of our problems

and in many ways in the 'here and now' they were
but then they just kept getting bigger and bigger
until we realized couldn't quite get away from
it and it was more so just the people in them

I:bid Suburban home looks out to the pure plush emptiness
of existence giving the safe and secure illusion of happiness
but if engaged in its dynamics will be deceived by the elements
of its expectations, while ironically, experiencing more so the patterns
(and phenomenon) of an emotional, psychological, and spiritual prison
than having anything to do with the concept of freedom or liberation…

These people get awfully territorial (and competitive) and what they do
to maintain becomes something of a terror with obsessive-compulsive behavior

I:bid All the talking and dreams that really
goes on behind the scenes of those ol' time
nostalgic muted home movies (self-advocacy
and overcompensating and 'animated' being)
which ironically in their simple and spare reality
appeared to hold so much more truth and meaning

I:bid

A closet discovered
full of those warped
water skis from when
they made those home
movies of human pyramids
at those summertime resorts
back in the 1950's wondering
where they are now probably
in one of those Upstate New
York towns no one heard of

I:bid Does it not seem as far back as the 1950's in America
(and still doing these exact same things on TV, in the movies
even TV commercials) they always got this frantic mass of
black & white frightened brainwashed people running away
from something. I'm so sick of these people running away
from things and wish they'd finally just tell us the reason
or who and what they are running away from? The exact

reason when I can afford it, always find myself traveling
to places like Sevilia, Switzerland, South of France, Sicily

I:bid Give me...

Your real nomads!
Your real madmen!
Your real drag queens!
Your real petty thieves!
Your real embezzlers!
Your real murderers!

These days everyone's self-promoting
and got their backers their audience
everyone believes in so much does
their tour and stopover and book
signing with Kathy Lee and just
one or more of the 5 or 6 late
night talk shows liked them
so much more when they
were undercover and
on the down low…

Jean Genet Sartre Bukowski
William Burroughs in Algiers
I mean was that Tangiers?
with a real genuine down home
problem with dope and the law

I:bid Is it just me, but does it not just seem like the media preaches
over our commercials and TV what it means to be holy and sacred
in America is to be obsessively-compulsively fit and aerobic where
some gung-ho overly-aggressive yuppie from hell in their tight stick
figure spandex is jogging through some steamy city street or scene or
what's supposed to be representative (because they are so no-nonsense)
of some dangerous ghetto (which will soon be gentrified and turned into
lofts and co-ops) up to the top of the pinnacle of the highest mountain,
omniscient, clinically-narcissistic, looking down on all of the universe
and honestly not sure (as if it would really matter) what they're doing
a commercial for? Gatorade? Some sneaker? Some car company who
just cares so much about the projected perfect all-American virtuous
lily-white Caucasian family because of course everything (in their
distorted thinking) still revolves around them with their privilege
and entitlement then show them taking that symbolic deep breath

representative of being so reflective and very single-mindedly
courageous, finding a way of attacking, conquering, stomping
back down the mountain, while you hear yourself saying out
loud 'Jeeze! What a bunch of fucken schmucks!' as whoops
just miss and crumbs from your babka fall deep into your
hairy chest and retrieve it and scoop it right back in your
mouth (why you call out to your wife who is heading out
to *Walmart* through the suburbs not by coincidence right
on top of the mountain, can you pick me up some wine?
and when she asks what kind you tell her it doesn't really
matter as long as you got your mental health) as just feel so
damn alienated and alone in this world by no fault of your own

I:bid Does rock & roll even exist anymore?
Elevator music? The last I remember
taking an elevator up in this fleabag
motel in Portland, Oregon hearing
the stray crooning of Country/Western
with all the leftover losers of civilization
nodding-out, negating their existence
all the drug addicts & drag queens
& runaways & killers, burnt-out
wasted after working the grave-
yard; least a good honest days

I:bid All these fake blondes in America
all with their very strategically placed tattoos
for purposes of seduction (their breast jobs…)
used to be something to be said about leaving
room open for the imagination yet in my opinion
eventually end up canceling themselves out and
looking exactly alike; not so sure about waking
up right next to a Barbie doll, maybe perhaps
if they provide a direction manual and 100%
money back guarantee if not fully satisfied

I:bid

15 bucks here
5 bucks there
35 bucks for
a fucken chap
book submission?

Kafka Kerouac
couldn't even
submit!
Mother
fuckers
getting
rich off
our shit
rather
purr
chase
a brand
new box
of *Topps*
baseball
cards with
those thin
sticks of
bubblegum
in them
and study
every last
one of
their
glossy
statistics!

I:bid Remember all the way back to childhood and all those acquaintances you grew up with and may have even been friends with suddenly deserted you and pretended like they didn't even know you for some strange reason until you find out with the passing of time and reflection and wisdom for the most shallow and pathetic and self-interested of reasons to be part of the infamous 'popular' and 'cool' crowd (how ridiculous that sounds now so aggressive and opportunistic at such young ages) and looking back what a clan of cut-throat conformist cowards while they conveniently abandoned ship and you remained on your solitary slow sailing raft of contemplation, kindness, compassion, and conviction, as think where all those great psychologists failed greatly such as Erickson with all his stages of "human" growth and development was that 'obscure and cruel' phase where one might have been forced into a sudden and unfortunate isolation or even situational depression without even being aware of it and to cope and survive and go it alone against those raging rapids (and if somehow make it through find they become far more independent and complete individuals perhaps even with far more insight, substance and wisdom)

Ibid: "The scapegoat" (often the one with true 'heart and soul,'
'down to earth' integrity or 'the individual') in the dysfunctional
family unit or child of an insensitive clinical narcissist will have
such a damaged self-image, identity, and sense of self-loathing,
feeling pathologized, a pariah, a clown or criminal, will go out
into their psychosocial environment, culture, society, everyday reality,
work world, and often without even knowing, reenact or parrot these exact
selfsame feelings in very much of a real life 'tragic self-fulfilling prophecy'

I:bid There are those with addictions
(with low self-esteem and identity)
who were criminalized originally
never given the opportunity who
put up the cities and communities
while the rest of the gentrified population
live off their hard work and labor somehow
paradoxically with that sense of privilege
and entitlement hanging out at cafes
with their lattes ironically alienating
like the world revolves around them
like they're the only ones welcome
these exclusive imitators of nepotism
who have all the time to pass judgment

I:bid What happens when you find out those who run the system
(the ceo's, managers, supervisors) with their connections and college
education, neighbors, the congregants, those at confession, the higher than
holy lady who sings in the church choir are all a bunch of compulsive liars?

(how they compartmentalize and rationalize
their phony and hypocritical lives...)

while you discover in the long-run it's really got absolutely nothing to do
with you, but how you decide to cope and survive with all these soulless
sleazy schmucks who never return calls or follow up or get back to you

I:bid Always hated that expression–
"I am not at liberty to say..."

Like who the hell was even asking anyway
as had absolutely nothing to do with liberty
and always seemed to come from that self-

important breed who had the need to flatter them-
selves like you were asking for some sort of favor

I:bid What's symbolic of symbolic as can guarantee
most great artists did not intend it but honestly were
just trying to survive or find ways to cope and get by;
the reasons why one kind of has to write satire or just
dreams at night or as Hemingway claimed with 'Old
Man and The Sea' was just trying to write a good story
or Bob Marley living the ghetto life with all the bullets flying
decried in brilliant broken Rasta 'all I can do is write love songs'

Any which way gonna find every which way to process you wrong

I:bid All that tranquil quiet and silence before the storm
if we could only get mankind down to that baseline
like after the circus leaves town; the life & times
of the jack-o-lantern and mini tree frog
perched on top looking all around.

The Holy Healing Scent Of Rain

Places i used to run away
as a teenage runaway from
port authority to places like
the jack london in portland
oregon a strange manifest
destiny where you'd meet
up with real-life prostitutes
actually becoming these mrs.
robinsons for fellow partners
and buddies but she really
did end up being like
a mom to us all
feeding us home-
cooked meals
and those days
where he ended
up feeling under
the weather would
take over and all
i had to do while
she was flashing
all the old men
in alleys from
the great north
west in case
they became
fresh was
to get out
the car and
beat the tar
out of them
never really
had to
and made
a percentage
in many ways
i really do miss
those days as
sincerely felt
like a family
and had meaning
in this supposed
up and coming
city you knew

so much
more a
bout up
and down
backwards
and forwards
always dappled
by damp miraculous
colorful watercolor
leaves with heaps
of hops from
the caged
corners
of midnight
mini breweries
licking off the
cobblestone
logs from
the lumbermill
moving down
the icy williamette
river mountain fogs
blanketed from heaven
you knew every thread
of which delicately
feathered the hills
of russet
& golden
& scarlet
& crimson
mixed mingling
with keen pungent
scents from that
deep lush forest
surrounding the
town after the
mad rain and
downpour came
crashing down
for its daily cleansing
ritual which in many
ways would heal and
wash away and liberate
your senses and take you
from melancholic to fantasy
to hopeful and able to function

once again to trainyards where
you knew other runaways actually
living in boxcars with books and bibles
black sons of real-life politicians and a
whole other panoramic view of the skyline
from the true ground up all those ominous
overcast bridges connecting downtown
to the ghetto which you knew inside
and out and when you were down
and out visited the phlebotomists
and places to donate your bone
marrow in case you were hard
up the 2 dollar movie theater
where stranded suburban
women neglected
by their salesmen
husbands always
out of town doing
god knows what
and so they
eventually
just decided
to give up
and end up
doing god
knows what
at the end
of that
thundering
lightning
pot of gold
at the end
of the rainbow.

Scenes From The Sunshine State

I always like when it's Hurricane Season in America and they interview
those natives who decide to just wait it out but never ever really provide
any real true clear or for that matter full explanation, but that they've
survived it in the past and it's become something of a tradition, and
what they've done the last couple of decades or so (some will even
look off with those faraway eyes and refer to this one or that one)
may even be holding onto some poor pitiful dog in their arms with
that sorrowful look of wisdom in their eyes, like they're the biggest
assholes and why can't they just this one time...and interview one last
pathetic poor soul with a scraggly white beard and nothing left to live
for holding onto his beer while the tide suddenly out of nowhere rises
roars picks them up hightop sneakers wifebeater and all and sweeps
them straight out to sea and miserably crazily wholeheartedly hollering
out something like–"Whoo-oopee! Wow-wee!" still holding onto that
beer in a brown paper bag pointing to the heavens and disappearing
to the horizon and can't help but to have a little respect for them
wondering if this is what they're talking about when they used
to refer to that custom and principle of American individualism?

Scenes From Inside Plato's Cave

Sitting back in your easy chair in the deep wee hours of the evening
like slipping in and out of a diabetic coma you come to the profound
startling revelation (not of the good kind) that you are still completely
hollow and really have not recovered at all from any of your trauma
and in instances like this learn to turn to the solace of just watching those
bright snake eye lights of truckers with their sappy Lincoln logs all tied
together on the back of flatbeds zooming and disappearing into the night
like when you used to runaway as a child from Port Authority and watch
the exact same kind of bleak beautiful reality just suddenly showing up
like some lost and long-gone miracle from nowhere in the middle of the
deep dark evening of The Mohave on your way to start a brand new life
out in The Tenderloin District of San Francisco and make a name for
yourself hooking up with the black market and all those hoods and petty
thieves you met on the back of the bus while also too escaping from The East
where you'd find yourself crawling up the outside pipes of whitewashed hotels
on Eddy Street like Rastas scaling palm trees to retrieve coconuts for free room
and board hollow like living in the last ramshackle home at the end of the board
walk at the end of the world in Coney Island with all the blind dogs & winos &
 ultra-orthodox Russian scholars hollow like being so tired can't get to sleep at
all after hustling a yellow taxi graveyard shift in New York City and the only
thing that will help me is the perfect melody of the melancholy mathematical
see-through sea through my screen window and static of sports radio and why
probably I used to just love to listen to The Smiths and Morissey like putting
some sweet ancient conch shell to my ear and hearing in awe the mellifluous beat
and rhythm and echo of the eternal shore from the beginning to the end of time
hollow like a piece of scorched driftwood washed up along shore which in more
ways than not *does* measure time as well as evolution and loss and folklore hollow
like just trying to get through the misery of the day to yesterday to tomorrow hollow
like a scooped-out piece of challah and all they leave you are the breadcrumbs hollow
like the pigeons and the bums hollow like living next door to the internal organs
of the last blast throng of foghorns when you got nothing left to live for and shake
and rattle your floorboards and bones and scare the hell out of you then make
you feel all safe and secure hollow with nothing left to spit-out and nothing
left to swallow hollow like hallelujah and how are you and not sure whether
it's a stray cat or kid screeching in the alley hollow like two poor poverty-
stricken boys going at it after school to defend their pride and honor and
prove or disapprove just to get approval and can't help but to head home
with their modest and humble bowed domes and downtrodden beaten
bones looking hurt and violated while no matter how tough they are sensitive
and compassionate to the core feeling criminalized when in fact they're all really
the criminals with all their brainwash and lies hollow just like Joe Buck at the
start of *Midnight Cowboy* before he takes off from that real-life dusty doldrum
town in downtown Texas to the madness of midtown Manhattan and to know
that not only is he hollow but so too are his flashbacks and the flashbacks

inside those flashbacks and guess in this real beatdown half-crazed fucked-
up existence you somehow managed to go out with some pretty wild women
who made you love and hate and question your reason for living but never giving
up and persevering having experienced marriage and an angelic child and got
your masters and a couple books published but still hollow! hollow! hollow!
hollow! hollow in measuring your mortality by all that has not been taken
or mistaken or sure as heck not misunderstood or misinterpreted so really
got nothing at all to do with being hollow while they're all just a bunch
of useless petty and moronic assholes (you can see it written all over
their face; what a disgrace, 'dis race!) as not the way was brought up
or trained but even if you are doing well how could you tell due to
their envy and jealousy and paradoxically get even more vengeful
and mean and nasty as the electricity comes back on in your home
and suddenly hear the moan of the country music station out of no-
where begin crooning–"crazy, crazy, crazy" with a bird on the wire
taking a crap and then taking off to the horizon hollow like one of
those stray roosters staggering on the side of some road trying to get
home but funny is right there on his own overgrown punch drunk lawn
as you head back to bed just like him hopefully not for more nightmares
but some good dreaming and porn and love and repeat to yourself like
some lost and found forgotten mantra made to keep away the madness
at least you reached your destination and made it up to the mountains
of Vermont like The Von Traps escaping Nazi-occupied Austria and
got a bit closer to the clouds and weather and God and Heaven
hell even if they don't get you and hollow as they come…

Motels And Stars Some
Where Behind The Smog

in the long run	nightmares
you realize	are simply
all you need	your subconscious
is a sink	giving you the silent
in the corner	treatment turning
to feed you	its back on you
fresh clean	ostracizing you
water for	from a culture
your episodes	you never ever
of insomnia	really wanted
when feeling	any part of
like a stranger	as if you
and returning	haven't
you to reality	seen enough?

Living Outside The Terrarium

i want to open up the first
dinner theater/funeral parlor
almost like those barber shops
they put in the halls of hotels
or at the bottom of subway
stations where they keep
the contented strangers
& those who get a thrill
or develop a real affinity
for our performances
& renditions of hair
& oliver & godspell
& les miserables
alongside our
fine gourmet buffet
surf & turf platters
& then if so choose
because feel
comfortable
enough with
the environment
just bite the dust
& very naturally
transition them
on some gurney
in the middle of
the performance
no less the wiser
as it's all about
bedside manner
& then dress
them up with
our award-
winning
makeup
artist
slash
em-
balm-
or
when
that
real-
life

or
pro-
verb-
yawl
curtain
falls
for
their
journey
& visit
to the
after-
world
becoming
something
of a custom
or tradition
as we all
know
there's
a fine line
between
acting
& reality.

The Cognitive-Behavioral Makeup Of Ghosts

1.

I want my ghost to make confessions
                         to be reflective...
     not like one of those who make loud obnoxious
                         declarative ptsd statements
i been through enough shit in my life
                why'd i want to hear this?
like poor clint eastwood's dog, lifelong companion
           who even he gets spit-on minding his own business

2.

I want my ghost
to be an exhibitionist
who flashes strangers
& opens up his trenchcoat
& where his heart & soul is
is some shattered snowglobe
& we'll find out who the real
true "innocent bystander" is

3.

I want my ghost to be a petty thief
and take back everything which
was stolen so surreptiously
to know the man of many
disguises ('dis guy this guy)
is the one who can separate
and tell the truth between the lie

4.

I want my ghost to be a real
true-blue host and one of those
old graying balding lounge singers
or some pathetic romantic, perhaps
in sequins playing with great conviction
and passion that ol' time billy joel classic

night in and night out–"i love you just the way
you are" in some beat down and lowdown bar

5.

I want my ghost to throw toasts
& riddles & roasts & then guess
if he must, vanish into thin air
like best friends & girlfriends
you were so fond of befuddled
& bewildered wondering
what you did to deserve
it becoming a former
ghost of yourself

6.

I want a room full of ghosts
until there are so many ghosts
you can never ever once again
possibly feel alone, until you once
more have a home, like one of those
wonderful corny elementary school
photos and the whole class all lined-
up in a double-decker row with great
big elastic smiles from ear to ear
frumpy hair, missing teeth, and
glowing eyes, like jack-o-lanterns
looking forward to the fearless future

7.

I want my ghost instead of being
some shocking stranger be a familiar
guardian angel keeping watch over
an extension to the senses separating
all worrying and things nihilistic from
the subconscious blue and melancholy
from all that which incapacitates us

8.

I want my ghost instead of being
some all-knowing schmuck be a
multiple-personality introverted
schitzophrenic, self-effacing
and modest, desperately trying
to figure out the ways of existence

9.

I want my ghost to be
a prattling protagonist
streetwise and intuitive
knowing the difference
between reality and risk
and rigid and resistance

10.

I want my ghost to have a social phobia
and be just as self-conscious as me
to be found mumbling to himself
while rounding the corner
on his way to his blind
date at the boxcar diner

11.

I want my ghost not be one of those
who loves the dust and clomping
chains and something of a hoarder
but a compulsive cleaner and demands
order and sweeps around with his mop
and pail of dirty filthy water to wipe
away all those devils who try to
bring about the doubt deception
denial and damage to an already
very fragile and erratic identity

12.

I want my ghost to be as disoriented
and distant as myself and not be able
to recognize his face in the mirror
pacing his floor in new orleans
suffering from that damn dsm
disorder tricalitimitia pulling
out his hair his eyebrows
his beard just to try and
come to terms with an
overbearing impossible
to please clinically
narcissistic awe
thor/itty figure

13.

I want my ghost to be a man of few words
again don't need all the bullshit and drama
and just stare out some foreign anonymous
train window a silent lonesome traveler
capturing contentment in the moment
realizing nirvana is just as fleeting
as the absurdity of existence

14.

 I want my ghost to look just like
one of those good ole wrinkled
fade/dead mugshots of someone
who's given up and tried it all
and just sick and tired of being
misinterpreted and underestimated
so becomes something of a fatalist
and whatever happens happens
as sure as heck put his whole
mind body and spirit into it

15.

I want my ghost to be a
multi-layered phantom
& every time you
peel off a new
layer of skin
there's another
one just a bit
more gentle
& delicate
& fragile
like some
angelic
child
whose
teeth are
chattering
out-of-control
due to the cold
& cruel weather
until you get to
the beautiful
& benign
skeletal system
which is the core
which is a warm
home-cooked
meal of leftovers
of pork chops
& baked
apples
& onions.

Bells & Steeples & Graveyards

i want to see the pristine lily-white swans
sitting around the garden table in their
whicker chairs at tea time with their
floral tea kettles and tea cups and
petite-fois and scones while old
women are doing the doggie paddle
flapping their arms and jowls elbowing
pushing each other out of the way just
to get to the breadcrumbs on shore and
the swans finally get up with their big bums
and arthritic bones and lament and moan and
groan about another long day done heading up
the twisting winding path at sundown to their very
safe & secure posh condos on the venetian blind horizon.

Something Like Pillow Talk

I.

Dear, i found the chocolate
babka from *grunenbaum's*
hidden in the lower daisy
wheel of the kitchen
and convinced
your mom
keeps on
sending it
to keep me
all fattened
for the season
like some poor
stuffed animal
secluded in hibernation
'cause of all the women
your dad cheated on her
with during their marriage
and subconsciously
subliminally forced
into a similar state of
controlled out-of-control
hoarding but no matter
it did help to heal
my melancholia
and left secret
babka crumbs
on the green
pea soup
saucer

II.

If you can
may you
ask her
to send
tea as well
specifically
from india
and that

delicious
addictive
english
twinings
that puts
you under
the influence

III.

There are reasons
why some men
might cheat on
their wives and
most of the time
it is not quite as
easy or obvious
or as much
of a crime
as you
might
very well
think, nigh
just for the sex
but something
spiritual, lost,
lonesome,
intellectual

IV.

Dear
i have a
confession
to make
and today
broke open
the almond
pleasure
and
chocolate
babka cake.

Okee-Dokey (Just Like Christ & Karaoke)

The literal last buffalo with an oxygen mask
strapped to his snout staggers across the plain
while across the way a convenience store with
a postcard carousel of everything which came
before and a strip mall of beauty salons with a
laundromat run by The Mob and an electrocuted

circus elephant just left in the parking lot for mistakenly
stomping a tourist to death for throwing cigarette butts
at him while the whole laugh track of Caucasians model
perfect cruelty and indifference and a certain sort of mock

Christian stingy good will competition when waves
from the old country come rumbling in carrying
needles and prophylactics and a veteran mowing
round and round the sign which reads "Confession."

At the end of the universe C. Columbus stands
on the roof of a tenement in Coney Island with
his faithful companion pit bull keeping an eye
out for 5-0 cuz all the way out in these parts
once again the economy has crashed
and needs a little cash to get ahead.

The wild animals from the twilight swamp
climb up the outside pipes of the YMCA
and try to slip into the steamed-up
windows just barely cracked open
attracted to the pungent aromas
of chlorine and bleach after the
janitors have mopped it all up

Perhaps even the milfs naturally
taking off their bathing suits with
their baby sons in the locker room
kind of making them all like angels

Jewish kids in night braces bloodshot brooding
about their future waiting in the darkening
dusk for their mothers to pick them up.

Fluorescent lights from the pool hall
and Alcoholic's Anonymous and bible
club will somehow lead them all home.

Joseph D. Reich

Dreaming Of Splendor When You're
Broke And Down On Your Luck

Sometimes you gotta just tempt fate
if it's sitting around being lazy all day.

Heck, I'd even take one of those *Cheap-O*
flights (50/50 get there alive...) just to get back
to my baseline and this time I'd really smell the roses.

Americana

i need one of those
   celebrity judges in my life
               not to be judged
                           & surely not celebrated
but on one of those blue melancholic days
       when i just might need a little validation
                     & share a few laughs & perhaps even
some secrets
& tea & scones
if that's not around
a moon pie or oreos
& when she takes off
in her sequins give her
one of those long mad
passionate kisses to
remember me by on
        one of those blue
                melancholic days
                       i'm not quite feeling right…

www.ingramcontent.com/pod-product-compliance
Lightning Source LLC
Chambersburg PA
CBHW080438170426
43195CB00017B/2812